"Noel Castellanos not only preaches and teaches on a holistic ministry of evangelism and community development, he embodies it. Noel's story, told through this timely and significant book, will encourage and challenge Christians everywhere to engage in the ministry of the hope of the cross lived out in the street. Through his life story, his ministry, his leadership of CCDA and now through this text, Noel Castellanos offers the possibility of a vibrant Christian faith not contained by the walls of a church building."

Soong-Chan Rah, author of *The Next Evangelicalism*

"The book reads like a modern day gospel story—it is very personal, intimate, engaging, challenging and through real stories of life presents the affirming and transformative power of Christian witness. It reads like a good novel, but it is profound theology at its best!"

Virgilio Elizondo, professor of pastoral and Hispanic theology, University of Notre Dame

"If you're tired of a disengaged Christianity, *Where the Cross Meets the Street* is the book for you. More than a book, it's an invitation to a journey of transformation and maturity. Noel, in sharing his own journey with us, calls us to a gritty and incarnational faith that forces us to see Christ in unexpected places. I found myself saying, 'Amen!' out loud. Every generation of Christians needs genuine street prophets—in Noel we have one."

Gabriel Salguero, president, National Latino Evangelical Coalition

"Part memoir. Part Bible study (in the best sense). Part training guide in community development. Part invitation to revolution. Noel Castellanos is one of the most influential leaders in the country guiding one of the most beautiful movements in the world, CCDA. I am honored to call him a friend and teacher . . . and many of us have been waiting for this book a long time."

Shane Claiborne, author and activist

"Noel is a leader of the times and a champion of the practitioner. This book takes twenty-five plus years of experience and gives us lessons and testimony to how CCDA brings the cross alive and makes it relevant today."

Leroy Barber, global executive director, Word Made Flesh

"*Where the Cross Meets the Street* reads like a novel. I couldn't put it down. With candor, humility and humor, Noel invites his readers to accompany him on his personal journey from obscure poverty to national prominence. The book is both emotionally touching and prophetically convicting. Inspiring."
Bob Lupton, author of *Toxic Charity* and founder of FCS Urban Ministries

"As someone who has ministered among the urban poor for the last fifteen years, this is the book I wish I had in my hands when I started. Noel Castellanos is an elite urban theologian, practitioner and dear friend to those on the margins. I have learned so much from Noel these past ten years and am thrilled he has accomplished the mighty task of putting his insight and experience into writing. My prayer is that this book will become incarnate in you as you incarnate the grace, truth and future of Jesus to those you serve."
John Teter, church planting team leader, Evangelical Covenant Church

"Any Christian leader in any city in the United States can draw biblical foundations and practical interventions from Noel's timely book. His story encapsulates the recent histories of the Christian Community Development movement and the diversification of leadership in evangelical America. This book is a must read for any leader plotting the engagement of the church in our culture over the next decade."
Rudy Carrasco, partnersworldwide.org

WHERE THE CROSS MEETS THE STREET

What happens to the neighborhood when God is at the center

NOEL CASTELLANOS

FOREWORD BY JOHN PERKINS AND WAYNE GORDON

IVP Books

An imprint of InterVarsity Press
Downers Grove, Illinois

InterVarsity Press
P.O. Box 1400, Downers Grove, IL 60515-1426
ivpress.com
email@ivpress.com

InterVarsity Press® is the book-publishing division of InterVarsity Christian Fellowship/USA®, a movement of students and faculty active on campus at hundreds of universities, colleges and schools of nursing in the United States of America, and a member movement of the International Fellowship of Evangelical Students. For information about local and regional activities, visit intervarsity.org.

Unless otherwise indicated, all Scripture quotations are taken from the Holy Bible, New Living Translation, copyright ©1996, 2004. Used by permission of Tyndale House Publishers, Inc., Wheaton, Illinois 60189. All rights reserved.

While any stories in this book are true, some names and identifying information may have been changed to protect the privacy of individuals.

Cover design: Cindy Kiple
Interior design: Beth McGill
Images: Outside urban mural: © Jeff Zimmerman/Jazim, Inc.
Dirty tire tracks: © Jamie Farrant/iStockphoto

ISBN 978-0-8308-3691-8 (print)
ISBN 978-0-8308-9756-8 (digital)

Printed in the United States of America ∞

Library of Congress Cataloging-in-Publication Data
Castellanos, Noel.
  Where the cross meets the street : what happens to the neighborhood
when God is at the center / Noel Castellanos.
     pages cm
  Includes bibliographical references.
  ISBN 978-0-8308-3691-8 (pbk. : alk. paper)
  1. Communities--Religious aspects--Christianity. 2. Neighborhoods.
3. Mission of the church. 4. Community development--Religious
aspects--Christianity. 5. Christian Community Development
Association. I. Title.
  BV625.C37 2015
  267'.13—dc23
                                                            2014044453

P 20 19 18 17 16 15 14 13 12 11 10 9 8 7 6 5 4 3 2 1

Y 31 30 29 28 27 26 25 24 23 22 21 20 19 18 17 16 15

To my Castellanos, Mendoza and Nicastro familia

Contents

Foreword

I (John) first met Noel in San Jose when he and his wife Marianne were living and working in the inner city. I invited him to come to Chicago for our first CCDA (Christian Community Development Association) conference at Lawndale Community Church. It was at this conference that Wayne first met Noel. Both of us recognized his heart for the hurting people of our world and his dedication to Christ and community with a desire to be an agent of change against the injustices in our world. A kindred spirit emerged immediately in our souls.

While at the CCDA conference Noel discovered the immigrant Mexican community of Little Village just south of North Lawndale. Noel returned home from our conference and talked with his wife Marianne about moving into Little Village and starting a church and a CCDA ministry. They both came to Chicago on a very cold, snowy December day with great resolve and enthusiasm to move to Little Village and begin. Soon after our encounter they moved their family to Chicago.

Noel has never missed a conference since, and Marianne has attended almost every one as well. Noel has helped us in the CCDA movement to understand the pain of Mexican Americans and other people of color who have been treated unjustly in America. Shortly after moving to Chicago, Noel came on the board of CCDA and began to have a voice among its leadership. Not long after that we asked him to be the vice chairman.

Noel's life experiences make him uniquely qualified to teach us and to write this book. Growing up as the son of immigrant migrant farm workers and now living in one of the largest Mexican immigrant communities in the United States, his perspective is remarkable. His personal involvements have also given him firsthand knowledge of prejudice, injustice and painful treatment as a Mexican American. We have been encouraging Noel to write this book for quite some time, and we are thankful that it is finally available as a tool for all.

The Latino voice is very important in the kingdom and in the CCDA movement. Those of us who have been blessed to know Noel have benefited greatly from his honesty and willingness to confront misconceptions and injustices with patience and love. Being the beneficiaries of a relationship with Noel, we have grown tremendously in our understanding of others living in the margins of our society. Noel helped us to move from a black/white association toward a more full expression of the American experience of Asians, Native Americans and Latinos, and being more inclusive toward the great diversity we have in America. His voice has been a tremendous asset to CCDA, the body of Christ and God's kingdom.

Noel has also been a leader in recent immigration issues, working tirelessly to help bring about solutions to this huge problem. His voice and perspective have been heard in the White House and Congress and among national church leaders and small groups of concerned Christians all over the United States. Noel has been showing justice and loving mercy and walking humbly with our God. He continues to show sensitivity and a tender heart of action to the disregarded of our society. For the last few years Noel has been a fantastic visionary leader as our CEO at CCDA.

Noel and Marianne are two of Wayne and Anne's best friends. We have been doing life together for over twenty-five years, with our families living just five blocks from one another. We are so thankful for their friendship.

We are sure that you will learn much and be encouraged to live out your faith in new and different ways by reading this book. Both of us love Noel dearly and thank God for his dedication to the Kingdom. Get ready to be taught, challenged and encouraged to walk with our Lord in a deeper, more meaningful way through Noel's story.

John Perkins and Wayne Gordon
Fall 2014

Mumbo Jumbo

In February 2012, I was in El Paso teaching a workshop on the principles of Christian community development at the invitation of one of our CCDA board members. I was thrilled to be near the border and was looking forward to crossing the Rio Grande to visit Juarez, Mexico, sometime during my trip. The event was being held in the basement of a hundred-year-old church in a very historic section of the city. Right before I got ready to start my presentation, I got a call from a friend in Washington, DC, informing me that one of our CCDA board members, Richard Twiss, had just suffered a massive heart attack, which took his life later that weekend. Though in shock, I went on to teach my session. When I was finished, I concluded my presentation with a passionate challenge:

> Like in the days of Nehemiah, it will take a group of pioneers overcome by a burden from God to incarnate our lives in the most vulnerable neighborhoods of our world, to see people's lives and neighborhoods transformed. And it will take the support, partnership and prayers of those who may not

sense God's call to move into a poor neighborhood but who are committed to seeing the shalom of God begin to emerge in every under-resourced neighborhood in our nation.

I asked the crowd for questions or feedback. Immediately, a woman seated in the front row, who looked old enough to be one of the founding members of this church, stood to her feet and shouted, "Everything you said is mumbo jumbo!" Wow! This was not how I expected our Q&A time to begin. After composing myself, I thanked the woman for her comment as respectfully as I could and went on to spend about a half-hour answering questions about my talk.

Since that encounter with the woman in El Paso, which was much scarier than anything I dealt with in Juarez, by the way, I have come to realize that when I talk about a more holistic approach to viewing the good news of the kingdom,[1] and our responsibility as Christians to be engaged in the most vulnerable neighborhoods in our nation, the approach I am advocating can sound a lot like mumbo jumbo. Broadening our traditional, evangelical paradigm of ministry (i.e., evangelism and discipleship) to include compassion, community development and the confrontation of injustice can seem too complicated, complex and messy. It would be so much simpler to cling on to the idea that regardless of people's race, culture or class—or whether we minister in Beverly Hills or in the *barrios* (Latino neighborhoods) of East Los Angeles—accepting Jesus is all that people need to live a great life.

I am aware that trying to wrap our heads around a different perspective can indeed sound like mumbo jumbo. But I am convinced that we can no longer maintain our old paradigms of ministry that compartmentalize and truncate the work of the kingdom and still make an impact in our world, which is in need of love and restoration. Broadening our understanding of the message and the work of the gospel can feel uncomfortable, to be sure. Almost treasonous.

Growing up a *Tejano* (a Texan of Hispanic ancestry), I loved football and the Dallas Cowboys. When I moved to California, I changed my allegiance to the San Francisco 49ers, who I still root for today. I am now surrounded by crazy Bears fans in my adopted city of Chicago, where I have lived for twenty-five years. Over the years the way I have come to read Scripture, and the way I have come to minister and live out my faith in the midst of extreme poverty and suffering, has often felt treasonous as well. But after living in poor Mexican barrios for more than three decades, seeking to be faithful to Christ, it seems less like treason and more like the appropriate next step in my understanding of the gospel of Jesus Christ.

In many ways this book is the story of how I have changed my allegiance from living for myself to attempting to live for the God who over two thousand years ago revealed himself *en carne* (incarnate) as a Galilean carpenter named Jesús. Many of you may struggle a bit with the Spanish I will interject throughout my writing, but I do so to give you a glimpse of the bilingual and bicultural reality of my life and context as a Mexican American in our mainstream American culture. In the pages of this book I hope to share how my upbringing, my education and everything else about my life have coalesced to shape my theological perspective and philosophy of ministry. Some of you will wonder why, in a book about ministry to those on the margins, you have to know my life's story. All I can say is, welcome to the world of *mestizaje* (the creation of a new people from two preexistent people), which is more comfortable telling stories like Jesus did than laying out rational theological arguments and propositions like the apostle Paul.

From the moment I began to seriously consider a new kind of

faith in the Liberator of the lost and the broken, who I encountered in the Gospels, I have felt torn and conflicted about the seemingly white, North American version of Jesus I was being challenged to follow. I assumed he was real, but if I was brutally honest, I was not certain why he would be interested in a kid like me from the border and the barrio. I figured I must have been chosen for some kind of celestial affirmative action program. On my way home from spending a week at the camp where I had a transforming experience with this Jesus, I remember having questions about whether he was as interested in me and my brown friends as he was in the rich white kids who made up the majority at camp.

Thankfully, through the influence and instruction of many mentors, authors and friends, I have come to the conclusion that it is precisely the men and women who have been overlooked and rejected by society who have a special place at the table of God's kingdom *pachanga* (rowdy celebration). Reading the Scriptures, I am overwhelmed to see how God consistently puts the neglected and oppressed at the center of his ultimate concern, not by targeting them as the objects of his salvific action but by redeeming and engaging them to be colaborers with the Holy Spirit in the mission of declaring and demonstrating to the entire world that the kingdom of God is at hand. This is exactly the good news that those of us on the margins have been waiting to hear!

Unquestionably, my path from the Texas border to the barrio of La Villita (Little Village) has been injected with the flavor of my *mestizo* (mix of Spanish and Native American ancestry) Mexican American upbringing and perspective. Yet my story is a continuation of the "Quiet Revolution" that John Perkins began to write about almost fifty years ago in the Mississippi Delta. In my estimation, what has made John Perkins' life and teaching so powerful is the fact that the biblically informed philosophy of Christian community development he has championed was developed from within the context of rural and urban poverty in the United States; that is, it has not been imported into our communities from the outside. Instead of imposing a theology and methodology on the poor, this movement has sprung up from the difficult soil of the 'hood and the barrio, which makes it authentic and relevant to our leaders and our neighborhoods. Today, I have the privilege and responsibility to steward this movement as the CEO of the Christian Community Development Association.

For a movement to survive with some variation of its original fire and fervor, it has to be owned, internalized and reimagined by and for each subsequent generation. This revolution of justice has been committed to building bridges of reconciliation across rivers of racial oppression and economic injustice as an expression of kingdom ministry, which is needed today more than ever before, not just in African American communities but throughout our entire nation: in Latino barrios and Native American reservations that have been consistently marginalized, in small cities left in ruins by the exodus of manufacturing, in rural areas forgotten and isolated by mass migration to urban centers, and even in suburban pockets of extreme vulnerability. I have dedicated my life to helping Christ-followers grow in their commitment to being present in these communities.

If we are going to be faithful witnesses to the message and mission of Jesus in vulnerable neighborhoods, we must expand our current paradigm of gospel-centered ministry to make certain that it puts the millions of people surviving on the fringes of our world at the center of our concern, because the margins are at the center of God's concern.

My prayer for this book is that you will find inspiration from my story, my ministry experiences, my theological insights and my own struggles to become a more godly and grace-filled leader. If you are investing your life by living and ministering in a vulnerable neighborhood, I pray that my honesty and transparency will encourage you to recognize the difficulty of our ministry context and convince you of the need to find other brothers and sisters who have a similar calling to walk with in your journey. For those who do not live alongside the poor but have a deep burden to love and serve others who have not experienced the kind of lifestyle that many of us have taken for granted in North America, I encourage you to reflect on my story and to continue learning about ministry on the margins, and then to get involved.

Finally, my hope is that Mexican Americans and other Latinos will feel affirmed and uplifted by my story. We need you to discover your God-given burden and to figure out how to engage authentically in the barrios of our nation and beyond. I also write with the hope that anyone who has felt exiled to the margins of mainstream Christianity and society can find solidarity with my struggle to discover an authentic faith, not in a white Jesus or a brown Jesus, but in the God turned Galilean, Jesus of Nazareth. Finally, I hope that you will discover another dimension to your faith in Christ and his mission on earth that is enriched by my Mexican American *and* Christian points of view.

Con mucho amor.

ONE

Mi Familia

This book is over fifty years in the making. Like the formation of everyone's ideas, mine have been shaped by specific events, circumstances and relationships. I am a third-generation Mexican American. I was born in 1959 to Anselmo Castellanos and Guadalupe Mendoza, just miles from the Mexican border in southern Texas. My parents were *campesinos* (farm workers), picking crops to feed our nation's families. To feed their own *familia* (family) my father worked in a factory that canned grapefruit and my mother worked as a beautician. They had two sons and two daughters. Both of my grandmothers had a lasting impact on my life. When my parents traveled the country to work in the fields, I stayed with Dad's mom, *Abuelita* (Grandma) Juanita. Her constant presence and love gave my life stability, and I loved her deeply. My mom's mother, Abuelita Chencha, died when I was only one. She was struck by lightning in the fields of Colorado as she ran for cover from the rain. I was cheated by her absence, as I needed all the love I could get. I was the oldest grandson on either side of the family.

Being a Tejano, my first language was a mix of Spanish and English. Like many US immigrants who are blessed to speak a second language, the moment I entered kindergarten I became bilingual. In fact, on the first day of parochial school my teacher in her "flying nun" hat changed my name. Instead of pronouncing *Noel Castellanos* like my parents and grandparents did, I left school that day with an Anglicized version of my name, which stuck with me until I arrived at college, like the sting from handling jalapeño peppers. At home, my name did not change, but I was developing multiple identities. I often felt like a piñata torn right down the middle by a kid desperate for his candy. I was neither Mexican enough nor *Americano* (from the US) enough, depending on where I was or who I was with. I was a *Pocho* (Mexican American) through and through. I was pure mestizo, or what Virgilio Elizondo calls a member of a new race born of the clash between Mexico, Texas and the United States. And living and existing between these worlds often created conflict in my soul.

In the 1970 Census, the Hispanic population in the United States was 9.6 million. (Of course, it was much smaller in 1959 when I was born.) According to the 2010 Census, that number has mushroomed to over 50.5 million Latino residents (16 percent of the US population). And over 63 percent of the US Latino population is of Mexican descent. Today, many demographers believe that by the year 2050, there will be 130 million Latinos living in our nation—with the majority of them being born in the United States. The browning of America is upon us, with unbelievable ramifications for our society, our politics and the future of the church. Recently, Latino journalist and TV personality Geraldo Rivera wrote *Hispanic Panic,* a book that adequately describes some of the trepidation that many US citizens feel when they contemplate this exploding demographic. The fear and concern that many in our country express regarding this unbelievable growth reminds me of the rapid growth of the Israelite population in Egypt:

In time, Joseph and all of his brothers died, ending that entire generation. But their descendants, the Israelites, had many children and grandchildren. In fact, they multiplied so greatly that they became extremely powerful and filled the land.

Eventually, a new king came to power in Egypt who knew nothing about Joseph or what he had done. He said to his people, "Look, the people of Israel now outnumber us and are stronger than we are. We must make a plan to keep them from growing even more. If we don't, and if war breaks out, they will join our enemies and fight against us. Then they will escape from the country." (Exodus 1:6-10)

Like most Mexican Americans, I was raised in the Roman Catholic Church. Growing up, all of my extended family members were Catholic as well, but I do not remember religion or faith being a significant factor in my early childhood. Faith and prayer, on the other hand, were huge for my diminutive, 4'9" Abuelita Juanita, who constantly prayed to Jesús and had great regard for the Church. One of my favorite stories about Abuelita Juanita is that when she reached retirement age, she asked one of my uncles to take her to the Social Security Administration offices near her hometown of Weslaco, Texas, to figure out what benefits she was entitled to. After looking up her social security number, the agent came back with bad news. "We have no record of you ever working or paying into the system." Her response was quick and furious. "¡Como que no he trabajado! What do you mean I have never worked? I have worked at home everyday raising nine children and taking care of my family. Of course I've worked!"

My six-foot-tall Grandfather Patrociño, on the other hand, was convinced that the Church's only intent was to take away people's hard-earned money. Thankfully, when I was just a few years old an archbishop came through our parish in Weslaco. Since I had been baptized as a baby in the church, I received my confirmation from the archbishop without having to attend any classes. I like to imagine it happened like it did in the movie *Rocky*, where his parents yelled up to the priest in his second-floor window, asking him to throw down a blessing for their son. I also faintly remember having dreams of growing up to be an altar boy. Looking back, I have no doubt that my religious upbringing began to shape my belief in God. A pale, white Jesus was everpresent in my home and in the church on crucifixes large and small. Paintings of this blue-eyed, surfer-dude-looking Jesus hung on the walls of almost every Mexican home I entered—along with JFK. Of course, Jesús was a common name for Mexican men (as common as Maria was for Mexican women). Religion was everywhere, but it would be many years before a personal and dynamic faith in Jesus of Nazareth would take root in my life and in the life of my familia. And it would be years before I would begin to question the reality of a white Jesus.

Although our family's faith was not deep or well-developed, we experienced the hand of God in our move from Texas to Northern California when I was around seven years old. An epic hurricane (Beulah) hit the Gulf of Mexico in September 1967 and devastated our small border town. Winds gusted at more than 160 miles per hour and forced the majority of residents of our small town of 10,000 to evacuate their homes. After being evacuated from our tiny wood-frame home, we, along with hundreds of people, moved into the massive city hall building, where we would be safe from the storm. In all, the storm caused over $1 billion in damage. Sometime during those horrid days my father made the decision to leave all of our relatives—grandparents, siblings, aunts, uncles and cousins—and move our family to California. As we loaded up our 1963 Rambler station wagon and hit the road with all of our family belongings, we were showered by heavy rains. The story goes that with great skill and determination, my dad tucked in behind a Greyhound bus, which parted the waters on Highway 10 all the way to California. I'm sure we thanked Jesús for his help on that day.

When we finally arrived in Northern California a few days later, weary from our journey west, we knocked on the door of my *Tía* (Aunt) Eva and her family, and they invited all six of us into their home—because that is what familia does. We stayed with our relatives for a few weeks, but it felt like a few months for everyone involved. Within a few weeks, my father, with his sixth-grade education, landed a great job at a General Motors factory, where he worked the night shift for years to come. It was a God-sent job that provided many blessings for our family, as well as the kind of pension years later that many of us only dream about getting today. Soon we found our own one-room apartment in a mostly Anglo-populated city twenty miles south of my relatives. We were excited to have work and a home, and we quickly realized we were not in Weslaco anymore!

Ironically, as we began our new life in Los Gatos (which means "the cats" in Spanish), I became keenly aware that although our city had a Spanish name, to be of Spanish-speaking descent was not looked on favorably. As strange as it may seem today with so many Mexicans and Latinos living in California, our family was a minority in our new neighborhood. I was quickly enrolled in an ESL class, where I worked hard and was extremely motivated to learn English. But no matter how well I seemed to make gains in my language skills, I was still the butt of my classmates' jokes because of the way I spoke English. On my way home from school I constantly encountered harassment and physical attacks. Needless to say, I worked extra hard to lose my accent.

Within a year my parents were able to save enough money for a down payment on our own home. Our entire family contributed to making this dream a reality. Every weekend we would travel south to Salinas or Watsonville, centers of agriculture, to pick strawberries or other crops in order to contribute to our housing fund. Truth be told, my two sisters, my brother and I squashed more berries with our rear ends than we put into the wooden crates we used for picking, but every little bit helped make the move into our new home a reality.

We realized we would never be able to afford to buy a home in the wealthy, white barrio of Los Gatos, so we moved to a city named Milpitas, which means "little corn fields" in Spanish. Apparently, years ago the place was filled with corn fields, but by the time we arrived even the apricot and walnut orchards were disappearing. Now, only apartments and track homes were sprouting up. Our new barrio was called Sunnyhills, and unlike Los Gatos it was diverse; many of our new neighbors looked and spoke just like us.

Sunnyhills was made up of working-class and poor families, mostly Mexican, Filipino, African American and mixed race. My best friend Frankie was half Mexican and half Guamanian. Regardless of our race, we were definitely united by our economic status and class. Most days, we probably did not know we were poor or lower class, except that almost everyone in our school received a free lunch from *Tío Sam* (Uncle Sam) and his government. Most of us qualified to stand in line to get USDA blocks of cheese and boxes of powdered milk, which everyone hated. We all made jokes about the two hundred ways to eat our welfare cheese. The few rich kids in our school joked that it helped our families afford to buy TVs and cars.

Fifth grade was pivotal in my life. My teacher, MaryJo Risse, was the most unique white person I had encountered. It turns out she had been married to a Mexican man in her past, and she had a daughter named Maria, who was half Mexican. MaryJo, who I am still in contact with after all these years, gravitated toward kids who were hurting, were underdogs, were from broken families and the like. She always found a way to encourage and love her students in that special way we all needed— kids like Frankie and me.

By the time I entered the fifth grade, Frankie and I were almost inseparable. We shared a love for all sports, especially baseball. We attended our first professional ballgame together—the Giants versus the Cincinnati Reds. We hung out after school. We rode our bikes around the neighborhood and spent many days playing music, golfing and hanging out with each other's families. We became more like brothers than friends. Frankie knew many of my struggles at home, and I was there when Frankie's mom and dad divorced during our fifth-grade year. I was also there with him a few years later when his mother died of a heart attack while she was still very young. MaryJo was constantly there for us throughout that year. Frankie needed a strong parental figure he could lean on as his family disintegrated.

Frankie struggled with confidence, and I know he wanted to blame himself for his parents' problems. I needed an encourager and a champion—someone who would express belief in me, as I grew up with a father who did not express love openly or provide emotional support. Growing up the oldest of nine kids and working at an early age to help his family survive, my father never received that kind of love from his own father. The older I got, the more I began to realize that my dysfunctional familia was not all that unique, but knowing that did not make it easier to endure. Unlike many kids, I knew who my dad was, and my parents were still married. But their marriage hung on by a thread, nearly unraveling hundreds of times during my growing-up years. Life was hell for Mom, and her courage and perseverance inspire me to this day. On many occasions I wasn't sure if she would survive the verbal and emotional abuse from my father, and it made me angry that she continued to endure her bad marriage. My sisters went to extreme measures to find love. They both ended up having children way too young, but they managed to become great moms. And my youngest brother, Rey, was too often left to fend for himself, yet he somehow grew up to be one of the most amazing human beings I know today.

Without someone like MaryJo stepping in to fill the void I felt in my life, I do not know where I would be today. MaryJo often noticed how distracted I was in class, not paying attention and lost in my own world. She often caught me drawing horses, cars and occasionally curvaceous girls like the ones I stared at on TV. I was punished and persecuted for my artwork quite a few times that year! Through all of my acting out, she saw I had a talent for drawing and creating, and she encouraged me. She affirmed me, and I began to feel loved. I began to feel like I might have a special gift that I could use in some way. Little did I know that years later I would complete a degree in fine arts (and I would be required to draw nude models in my painting classes in order to complete my degree!). Incredibly, MaryJo and my parents were present at my college graduation long after my life-changing year in fifth grade. Although back then she didn't talk much about God, she did possess a Christlike, gritty, unconditional kind of love that compelled her to give unusual attention to her students with very deep needs—students like me.

The kind of hands-on involvement that MaryJo provided for Frankie, me and many other kids in Sunnyhills is exactly the kind of incarnational love that is so desperately needed in neighborhood schools across our country. Our Chicago public school system serves close to 500,000 students—mostly from vulnerable African American and Latino communities. Teachers like MaryJo often become the ministers who walk with these children every day, not only working to provide them with a quality education but also becoming their mentors, counselors and surrogate parents, often with little support, fanfare or appreciation.

I can hardly imagine surviving my elementary years without MaryJo. Even though she knew the important role she was playing in many of her students' lives, she also recognized the importance of not trying to replace our parents. Instead, she came alongside them when possible to add another strand of love and encouragement.

My father worked on the assembly line at General Motors for close to thirty years. Like most of us who are fathers, he failed to be the perfect dad, but he was a strong provider for his family. He would never hear the crowds cheering him for a job well done. I'll never forget the day he was the center of attention in my fifth-grade class and how that made both of us feel.

In her bold way, MaryJo took quite a risk inviting her students' parents to class to share about their professions and careers without asking us about it first. For certain, we would have done everything in our power to make sure it never came to pass. It was one thing for Frankie's dad, who was a NASA engineer, to share about his work, but what in the world would my father have to say about his job installing windshield wipers on the GM assembly line? This would be the most embarrassing day of my life!

When the day arrived, I wanted to pretend to be sick, but I knew better. I saw my father pacing nervously outside of our classroom. I'm sure he was as worried as I was terrified about his upcoming presentation. He shyly made his way to the front of our class and had every eye staring at him. MaryJo stood by his side, trying to ease his nervousness, and introduced him to my class-mates. It was one of the most spectacular introductions that I had ever heard. You would have thought she was introducing someone who had found the cure for cancer. When she came to the end, her final punch line was "Can you imagine what the world would be like if we had to drive our cars in the rain without windshield wipers?" The entire class went nuts, and my dad left that day feeling loved; he was affirmed in a very Jesus-like way. Imagine if children and parents in every US school located in tough neighborhoods had a teacher like MaryJo!

Miraculously, I survived junior high, my first real girlfriend crushes, my Jesus-like long hair and an attempt at acting in drama class. I quickly reasoned that I already had enough drama in life, so I quit. By the time I entered high school my art was showing promise and I was becoming a pretty good athlete. I participated in football, baseball, soccer, tennis and golf, but I felt emotionally beat up by my family life. My parents continually seemed to be on the verge of getting a divorce. As the oldest child, I took on too much pain and too much responsibility, often blaming myself for their problems. Amazingly, in my junior year, with the generous and surprising help of my father and with some money I earned selling eight-track tapes of Motown hits at the flea market, I was able to buy a bright orange 1969 Firebird. It was amazing. No more walking to school. No more bumming rides. Life was looking better.

Not long after I started driving my car to school, I offered one of my classmates from the neighborhood a ride home. He was a nice dude, but we weren't close friends. In fact, he was a bit of a Jesus freak who always toted a huge, family-sized Bible wherever he went. He was one of the first non-Catholic Christians I knew, and he would often tell me that God loved me. After arriving in California, my family only attended church on occasion—midnight mass on Easter and Christmas, with a few funerals thrown in. Some of my friends and their families attended the Catholic Church as well, but none of us were in danger of being called Jesus freaks. At the time, church and Jesus were as irrelevant as eight-track cartridges are today.

When my friend got into my car, he began to compliment me on my new ride. He went on and on about the great paint job the car had. He made comments about how clean the interior was— so black and shiny. Then he asked me about the engine, which was in pretty bad shape. Before he got out of the car, he made a comment that I'll never forget. "You can have a car with a great paint job and shiny interior, but if your engine is no good, you've got problems." He got out of my car and walked away.

I'm not exactly sure how, but as soon as he left, I knew he was not only talking about my car. I could sense in the deepest part of my being that he was talking about my spiritual life. My life seemed pretty good to many of my classmates and friends. Even though I had family problems, I had a car. I was a good athlete with lots of recognition. My grades were good. I had lots of friends who, besides getting me to smoke dope and drink too much beer, were good guys. I had a few opposite-sex relationships that served to ignite and activate all of my teenage hormones. Yet none of these relationships seemed to fill the void I felt in my heart. Surprisingly, by the end of high school, I was not addicted to drugs or to finding romantic love, but I was beginning to realize that I needed help figuring out what was missing. Like my car, my life and my heart were in need of a new engine—one fueled by the unfailing love of God.

That help came from an unexpected place. My history teacher and football coach, Bob Kellogg, had a way about him that made his students eager to learn about the Great Depression, about blitzing linebackers and about the story of God invading planet Earth in the person of Jesus. While I had very little in common with Mr. Kellogg, his love and concern expressed in the time he invested in his students made him someone I wanted to hang around. I was not alone; many other students felt the same way. His dry sense of humor, his corny jokes that broke up the monotony of class and his ability to get us to think and learn made him a great teacher. During my sophomore year, Bob's powers of persuasion stirred an interest in a few of us to attend a summer camp, one with horses, motorized minibikes and lots of girls!

That Young Life camp's hefty registration fee was a challenge for some of us barrio kids. But weekend after weekend our small posse of friends washed cars, did odd jobs and raised the money we needed to get to camp. Our parents helped us, but Mr. Kellogg was right in the middle of all of our fundraising efforts. By now my parents were very bilingual and felt pretty comfortable speaking English in public. They spoke much better English than I spoke Spanish. Like the characters in Julia Alvarez's book *How the Garcia Sisters Lost Their Accent*, I worked hard to lose mine, and I felt like an Americano with brown skin who liked tortillas, tamales and *menudo* (Mexican soup), but who was not like the real Mexicans I knew in our barrio or back along the border. Somehow my brown skin and love for my mom's authentic Mexican food did not magically translate into an ability to speak fluent Spanish. On our occasional trips back to Texas to visit my grandparents, I had to put what little Spanish I did speak into action or I got no tortillas.

Once we arrived at this rustic but beautiful camp in the Gold Rush Country of California, I was bombarded with smiles and kindness from the staff, and with unfamiliar God-talk from the Bible. The middle-aged white speaker that week wore jeans and a T-shirt when he talked about God. When he stood up to speak, he held a very small, multicolored Bible unlike any I had ever seen before. During club time, we would hear about a new episode in the life of this Jesus, who I still suspected was white, and afterward we would go back to our individual cabins to talk about what we'd heard. Mr. Kellogg told us there are no stupid questions, but, we jokingly added, only stupid people. These club meetings and discussion times were becoming almost more important to me than the fun and games we had each day. I was conflicted because we had come to camp ready to party and to score with the girls, not to get religion. My friends and I came with enough weed and alcohol to party all week, and one of the guys even brought a very large box of condoms he stole from his father. We all joked and bragged we would take the box home empty.

By week's end, a huge tension was forming in my heart. The more I listened to the story of Jesus and his love for me, the more I felt drawn to this man with superhuman powers who claimed to be God. That week, spent away from the craziness of my family, I had the space to explore my faith in a way I never knew was possible. On the final night of camp, after our nightly cabin discussion, we were challenged to spread throughout the property in total silence, and to speak simply and directly to the God we had been learning about all week. My experience that night was scary and sacred at the same time. Much of my time was spent looking at the millions of stars in the pitch-black sky and reflecting on the love of God.

The idea that God bridged the expanse between heaven and earth in the person of Jesus to show me his love was mind-blowing. At the same time, I was also flooded with anger toward my dad. Even more painful than my anger toward my father was the realization that my heart was a mess and that I was longing for a love I wasn't sure even existed. Before this week I was beginning to believe that I was special and gifted and loved, as MaryJo had begun to show me in the fifth grade. I was also painfully aware that my heart was filled with sin, hate, guilt and sorrow. I needed forgiveness, and I desperately needed to learn to forgive. Now I was being told that this Jesus, who I'd known about all of my life, was the answer to healing my heart and, possibly, to giving a new start to my relationship with my father.

Later that night the entire camp met one final time to sing and to celebrate a week that changed many of our lives. Toward the very end of our club time, the speaker, Bob, who is still a friend to this day, asked those of us who had prayed to invite Jesus into our lives to stand up and say so in front of everybody. Afraid and very self-consciously, I somehow mustered up the courage to be the last person in the room to stand up that night to declare that I was going home with Jesus in my life. My friends were shocked, but not as shocked as I was to be taking this bold step of faith. This experience would shape the direction of my entire life.

Both MaryJo and Bob had a huge impact on my life. Not only did they instill confidence in me in their unique ways, but they both modeled for me the importance and power of relationships. The ways that they entered into my world to demonstrate that they cared for me and my friends taught me that getting involved and investing in people's lives can truly make a difference. They also helped me break my stereotypes of white people. Now, Jesus was also entering into my world. I knew I needed his love, but I still had much to learn about who he is and about the plans that he has for my life.

TWO

Leaving the Barrio

About the time I was moving to California with my family, John Perkins was also making a move; he was leaving California to return to Mississippi after feeling a call to return home with his newfound fervor for God. The story has been told many times about how his son Spencer invited John and his family to attend church after getting involved in a Good News Club. For John, a newfound faith in Jesus and intense discipleship followed, which ignited a deep burden for preaching the gospel with the power to break down the strongholds of poverty and racism.

Once he returned home, he began the work of building a church and of rebuilding a rural community drained of resources and leadership. It was the zenith of the civil rights era in the South, and the divisions between blacks and whites were as wide as the Mississippi River itself. While John set out to establish a church with a zeal for evangelism and discipleship that reconciled people back to God, it quickly became apparent that a new approach was needed. Along with offering hope for eternity, it had to be rooted in the current struggles of his neighbors who lacked jobs, adequate health care, educational opportunities and relief from the oppression of postslavery Jim Crow laws. It wasn't enough to move people emotionally in church as a way to forget their problems; faith demanded working and praying to bring about justice in the here and now.

The more John examined and assessed the situation in Mendenhall, Mississippi, the more he became convinced that unless he and his wife, Vera Mae, were able to develop leaders to love God and to take ownership of the vision to see their neighborhood transformed, their mission would not be complete. In order to develop these leaders, he reasoned, their young people had to get an education and then relocate back in Mendenhall to be agents of the kingdom with the new skills they had gained.

Economic empowerment was at the heart of John's vision as he established the new work in Mississippi. With his experience and success as a businessman in California, he knew that true freedom for the families in his community had to include stable jobs and the opportunity to own their own businesses. Charity had to be replaced with development in order to truly set people free. John knew that while it was good to give a man a fish so he could eat for a day, and that it was better to teach a man to fish so he could eat for a lifetime, what the people in his community really needed was help finding their way to own the pond. This way, they could have control of their own economic destiny. Building relationships to attract resources and then redistributing them into the community to create opportunity and sustainability was critical to his strategy, and it ultimately attracted greater investment for their community revitalization efforts. This example of holistic development based on reconciliation, relocation and redistribution became my inspiration for ministry in the years to come.

In a similar way that John was sending young leaders to further their education in Mississippi, I was being encouraged to apply to college by my coach and mentor. Coach Kellogg had earned my trust in high school. Along with taking me to camp, he hired me to help him and his wife Deni build their home even though I knew nothing about construction. The summer work provided me with a job and gave him the opportunity to keep teaching me the basics of the Christian faith.

I was most affected by watching how he treated his wife with love and respect, which was so different from what I experienced at home. For two years, a few friends and I would go to Coach's house every Saturday morning to have breakfast and to study the Bible. Even though I was really struggling to live out my faith, I was convinced I needed Jesus and was committed to learning more about God. I'll never forget the morning we read the story of King David and his *loco* (crazy) shenanigans. I was shocked to see this guy who really loved God mess up so badly. With a little too much time on his hands, he took a peek at a beautiful married woman, Bathsheba, bathing naked on her roof. Even though he was a man after God's own heart, he abused his power and had this woman brought to his palace to have sex with her. He got her pregnant and then devised an elaborate plan to make it seem that she got pregnant by her husband, who was a leader in the king's military. Unbelievably, King David arranged to have Bathsheba's husband killed to cover up his sin, and he then took this woman as his wife.

Wow! I had never done anything that outrageous, and I could not believe this stuff was in the Bible! I knew there were some wild stories in the Bible about Jesus turning water into wine, controlling the weather and even raising his friend from the dead, but this scandalous story read like a made-for-TV Mexican *novela* (soap opera). I was beginning to see that if a man like King David could love and serve God, then maybe I could as well. However, I needed a change to jump start my struggling faith. I seemed to be stuck.

Late in my senior year, I got acceptance letters from the three colleges I applied to: UC Santa Cruz, Seattle Pacific University

and Whitworth College in Spokane, Washington. My first incli-
nation was to stay close to home and attend school in the hills of
neighboring Santa Cruz, where I had driven many times to party
with my friends at the beach and boardwalk. I knew I wanted to
study fine arts but wasn't too sure about much else. As I was beginning to settle into the decision to stay close to home, Coach
Kellogg and another Christian teacher at my school encouraged
me to consider attending a Christian college. Both SPU and Whitworth were small, Christian, liberal arts schools with good art
programs, and I began to get excited about the possibility of
getting a brand-new start far away.

I had never been in the state of Washington and did not make
a visit to either school as I considered my decision. I really don't
know how my parents and I got through filling out financial aid
forms, but I assume we had help. Knowing how confusing it is
to fill out the FAFSA student aid forms for my own kids today, it
was truly a miracle we got through that process. As the time
came close to decide on a college, I talked through my options
with Coach Kellogg and my parents. I could go to SPU, where it
rained a lot, and I could play soccer. Or I could go to Whitworth,
where it snowed, and I could play on the tennis team. I was so
superspiritual at the time, the deciding factor for me was wanting
to experience the snow. Little did I know that years later I would
end up living in the snowy, cold tundra of Chicago.

Leaving home and arriving at Whitworth, which was neither
ethnically nor culturally diverse, were both sizable adjustments.
At the school there were a few African American guys on the
basketball team, a small number of international students from as
far away as Saudi Arabia, and a sizable number of students from
the islands of Hawaii. (I later found out that a Whitworth alumnus
returned home to Hawaii and began to send kids to Spokane. I
was always amused to see these guys wearing flip-flops in the

middle of winter, pretending the snow was hot white sand!) I was assigned a dorm room with two guys from the islands. One was a superfriendly, somewhat eccentric guy with a pet ferret; the other was a high-strung premed student who already knew he wanted to be a dentist. Even though I was not Hawaiian, I was close enough.

Years later, Christian colleges and universities across the nation continue to struggle with a lack of diversity. These institutions, who fancy themselves as the developers of tomorrow's Christian leaders, are unfortunately not seen as places where nonwhite students can flourish and excel. These students often find themselves isolated and marginalized on majority-white campuses. These schools have a difficult time affirming the experiences and cultures of others. For over thirty weeks of the school year the dominant culture is celebrated and extolled by a constant parade of white speakers, white professors and white leadership. Only a few weeks are dedicated to acknowledging the existence of Latino and African American cultures and leaders. In terms of diversity, the evangelical community is far behind the rest of society.

I have been pleased that in the last few years a few Christian colleges around the nation, including Whitworth, are attempting to take steps to be more inclusive. Through the development of programs like Act Six, initiated by Dave Hillis and his team in the Pacific Northwest, a cohort scholarship model is supporting nonwhite students from underresourced neighborhoods to integrate into Christian colleges with greater intentionality and support. This kind of initiative is smart for colleges that increasingly are struggling to reach enrollment goals. Universities that are seen as embracing young men and women from diverse ethnic and economic backgrounds will have an advantage when recruiting these students.

Recently, I began to serve on the board of trustees for Warner Pacific College in Portland, Oregon. They not only have Act Six students but have made it a priority to promote the city's urban reality as a key selling point for the college. In the last few years I have been privileged to meet some of Warner's dynamic, young Latino students. These students are taking leadership roles on campus and are an example of what we can expect from young men and women of color who are welcomed into our university communities. If teachers like MaryJo and Bob, who helped guide me as a student, could point their students with confidence to colleges and universities who embrace nonwhite students, attending Christian colleges would not be as much of a challenge.

Being in Spokane was a culture shock. It was a small city, with mountains and rivers and lots of green everywhere. As far as I was concerned, Whitworth was totally isolated from civilization, even though it was just at the outer edge of town. I missed the diversity of California and the urban vibe of the Bay Area, and a Mexican was hardly to be found, not at school, not in town, not anywhere. And the only burritos I could get my hands on were from Taco Bell. I finally met a young woman on campus with a Spanish surname who insisted she was not Latina. I guess she was still working through her identity issues, which I understood. Eventually, I discovered that there was a *Chicano* (Mexican American) brother from Colorado on the football team. I never got to know him well during my four years at Whitworth, but I was glad to know he was around. As I was adjusting to my new surroundings, I desperately missed my friends and family and often felt like a fish out of water so far away from home. This is a common experience for many minority students who must work to adjust to an environment with very little diversity.

During my time at Whitworth, many students and faculty complained that it was becoming too liberal. I, however, had never been around so many Christians in my entire life, so I didn't know the difference. I was just learning the distinctions between Presbyterians, Pentecostals and Roman Catholics. Before long, I was attending a church connected to the Foursquare denomination, which I knew nothing about, with a young pastor I really liked. So here I was, a Catholic kid from the barrio living in Spokane, attending a Presbyterian college and worshiping at a charismatic church.

Without question, one of the most significant decisions I made when I arrived at Whitworth was to introduce myself as Noel Castellanos—with the Spanish pronunciation I had lost in kindergarten. I figured it was time to reclaim that part of my fading identity as I launched into the future as a Mexican American college student very far away from the barrio.

Over the next four years, I would throw myself into my art. I loved my drawing and painting classes, and I had professors who pushed me to develop my skills and my own artistic point of view and style. I also had an amazing time playing on the tennis team with an iconic coach, Dr. Ross Cutter, leading the way. On road trips throughout the Northwest, I always took the entire rear seat of the fifteen-passenger van that carried our eight players. Coach Cutter would count everyone in the van to make sure he never left anyone behind, and when he got to me, he would yell *"ocho"*—number eight in Spanish—trying to impress us all with his bilingual skills.

Before long, my days were filled with dorm activities, making new friends, studying art and playing tennis whenever it wasn't snowing. And I detected a spark in my spiritual life that I had never experienced before. One of the most compassionate and caring people I had ever met, Dana Schilperoort, became one of my roommates my sophomore year. Ironically, although he attended a different high school than I did in San Jose, Dana had been at camp with me the summer I started my walk with God. That entire year at Whitworth we had long talks about our faith and what it means to love and follow Christ. Dana had spent the previous year living and studying in Latin America, so he had a very unique and distinct perspective from anyone I knew. Sadly, this *gringo* (white person from the US) spoke Spanish much better than I did. We talked about his love for Latino cultures and about the many injustices he saw in Latin America that he was convinced were perpetuated by US foreign policy. Whenever he greeted me, he would yell "*vato*," which is barrio slang for "dude." This made me feel right at home.

Along with studying art, I decided to take a few religion classes in my second year. I completed a fantastic class on the Gospel of Matthew, taught by Dr. Dale Brunner, and a New Testament theology class, taught by Dr. Roger Mohrlang. Both were stellar Christian men and excellent teachers, and I became fascinated with the Bible. Much of what I was learning was not as exhilarating as the story of David and Bathsheba, but it was every bit as exciting because I was discovering the story of God for myself. I was still not a strong believer, but changes were slowly taking place in my life that I never thought were possible.

My most significant passion during my time in Spokane was working with youth. I volunteered with the local Young Life ministry, helping nonchurched kids like myself discover the love and forgiveness of Christ. Although I was able to fit in a few casual relationships with some young coeds, I discovered that ministry was beginning to capture my heart.

Week after week I was getting sucked into my volunteer work with students at Lewis and Clark High School. I had the privilege of working with a wonderful team of leaders from a variety of walks of life. Of course, I was the only Mexican American on the team. Before the end of my first year as a volunteer leader, the staff person who supervised our work announced that for the next year he was going to appoint a young woman named Heather and me to colead the club ministry at Lewis and Clark. In a very profound way this motivated me to take my faith much more seriously. I did not want to mess things up for Jesus, for the kids or for my team.

By now, I was very aware that all of the Christian leaders I was being exposed to at Whitworth and in my Young Life ministry were white. The only exceptions were my Hawaiian roommates and two Mexican American guys who became great friends—one a grad student and the other a brother from East Los Angeles who moved to Spokane to work and to escape the barrio. I was excited about my growing faith and my budding ministry work with youth, but I longed for contact with other leaders from the 'hood, the barrio, who were serious about their faith and had leadership responsibilities in ministry. Because all I saw in positions of Christian leadership were white men, I began to believe that Mexican Americans might not be expected or qualified to lead. I hoped that I was wrong about this.

I remember like it was yesterday the first time I gave a fifteen-minute club talk at the start of my junior year. Our leaders worked hard to invite hundreds of students who were slowly becoming more than just acquaintances. I could not believe that I was now trying to love these kids the way Coach Kellogg loved me. The night of club, over a hundred students jammed into the humungous home of one of our young women. We played stupid, crazy games that the kids seemed to love, sang some songs in a manner that probably bordered on sacrilege for those from a traditional church background, and then I stood up to give my talk. Many of the kids already knew me, but this was my first time in front of the group with a Bible in my hand. To hook the kids, I told them a story about trying to impress a girl with my '69 Firebird, and how it did not go well. I also told the story of Peter and his short-lived attempt to walk on water. I went on to say that during the school year we hoped to introduce them to the man Jesus who was like nobody else in history, with the hope that they would come to discover, like I had, that he is God.

I was very nervous during my talk and was relieved that I didn't choke. Afterwards, many of the students came up to harass me about being dissed by the girl in my story and to thank me for my talk. Somehow, I had connected with these young people, and it felt good—similar to the first time MaryJo expressed that I was gifted at drawing. My team leaders affirmed me as well, giving me the courage to envision the possibility of speaking again, which I did many times over the next two years.

Learning to identify with the youth in my club was a stretch for me because the majority of these kids were wealthy and white. I worked hard to find ways to connect my story to theirs, except where it came to sharing my family pain. Many of these seemingly perfect kids were struggling to feel loved by their parents, or they felt alone. Many of them had all the toys that money could buy, but they seemed to have the same hole in their heart that I was longing to fill in my own life.

Before too long, I became aware of a group of Laotian refugees who began to attend Lewis and Clark High School and definitely needed friends. They were practically invisible and ignored by all the students at school, even by the kids attending our club. I found myself drawn to these young men and women who existed on the margins of the school's mainstream, so I began to look for ways to enter their world. I was used to being the outsider and wore that honor like a comfortable, warm coat; now these Laotian youth were getting the cold shoulder on a daily basis without much hope for meaningful relationships on the horizon.

By the end of my senior year in college, I was in a serious relationship with a young woman from the west side of Washington State that eventually came to a painful end. I began spending most of my free time meeting with students, planning club meetings, preparing evangelistic talks and rounding up these kids to go to a fabulous camp in British Columbia. Camp Malibu was a spectacular place hidden between snow-capped mountains that could only be accessed by ferry, and I finished my final summer of college taking a group of my club kids to experience one of the best weeks of their lives. They not only had an amazing week experiencing the fun and beauty of Malibu, but many of them began a new walk with Christ, the same way that I had done just a few years before.

Somehow, I completed my degree with a double major in fine arts and biblical studies, and was contemplating what I would do after graduation. The answer came late in my final semester, when I was invited by the Young Life staff in the Bay Area to attend a national Urban Young Life conference in the Mission District of San Francisco. I didn't realize it then, but my future wife, Marianne, was at that conference; she was working with urban kids in Nashville after graduating from Vanderbilt University. I was also thrilled to finally meet some African American and Asian American staff at this conference—although I could not find another Mexican American besides myself.

A few days after returning to Spokane, where I was completing final projects and beginning to say goodbye to my Young Life leaders and kids, I received a call from the western divisional director, Tom Raley, inviting me to join the staff of Young Life in San Francisco as a part of their new Urban Initiative. While I had some concerns about working in this organization with so few non-white leaders, I knew that working with urban youth is what I was supposed to do—and I was thrilled to have a job! How I'd gone from a young vato living in the barrio of Sunnyhills to becoming a full-time Christian youth worker in San Francisco was puzzling to me, but my new adventure was about to begin.

THREE

A New Burden for the Barrio

Arriving in San Francisco as a college graduate to start a full-time job as a youth worker felt surreal, and in no way did I feel ready for this assignment. Although San Francisco was just fifty miles north of where I grew up, and was a place I had visited dozens of times over the years to watch baseball games and visit the wharf, this time when I drove my red VW Beetle into the city it was different. As a trainee in this new Urban Initiative, I was definitely the rookie on the team, along with a few other trainees. Apparently, I was joining one of the elite Young Life urban areas in the nation led by an ex-Texan (and Governor Rick Perry look-alike) area director named Dale Vollrath. Dale was a tough, no-nonsense leader who was well-respected and feared by all. It seemed he had achieved the impossible in San Francisco in terms of making Young Life a relevant and well-funded ministry.

My assignment was to work under the leadership of seasoned and streetwise African American brother Michael Thurman, who was married to a white woman. He was a talented and caring leader with a great big heart for high school kids. I was also paired to work with a trainee, Richard Acevedo, who was half Mexican. Richard and I decided to find an apartment together in the Mission District, which was the center of the Latino community in the city. Unlike San Jose, where I had grown up, the majority of residents here were from Central America, not Mexico. Although the Spanish language and mestizo features of the people were very similar to Mexicans, the culture and food of my Salvadorian and Guatemalan neighbors were quite unlike anything I had encountered. Instead of eating tacos, I was learning to eat pupusas, a Salvadorian dish very similar to Mexican gorditas—corn tortilla-like shells filled with cheese and meats—which were delicious! To spice things up even more, the outer Mission was also home to a huge population of Filipino Americans. Hipsters had not yet invaded this neighborhood, as they have today. It was adjacent to the Castro District, which is still one of the largest and most well-known gay communities in the nation. The clashing of these distinct cultures in one of the most densely populated cities in America made for an unbelievable adventure for a twenty-two-year-old recent college graduate.

The Castro District was one of the first gentrified neighborhoods in the city. Back then I had no idea what gentrification was. But I had a front row seat to witness the gradual transformation of this neighborhood. As middle-class gay men moved in and bought and rehabbed beautiful, old Victorian homes in the community, which had been cheap flophouses for the poor, these homes became more expensive. Absentee landlords began to see the gold mine they were sitting on, and instead of continuing to rent their places to Central Americans and other men and women struggling to get by, they began to cash in. The more homes were turned over to more financially secure residents, the higher the taxes increased. This forced the few homeowners that were left in the neighborhood to sell their properties. Gentrification was alive and well.

The entire team was impressive and incredibly diverse for an evangelical ministry in the early 1980s. Along with my African American supervisor and our Texan boss, the staff was composed of a Chinese American brother, a couple more African Americans, a Native American woman, who became a good friend, and a few Anglos. All lived within the city limits. Our team had amazing and unique personalities that remind me of the eclectic crew of the *Ocean's Eleven* movie—only instead of pulling off heists for money, we were all determined to make an impact for the kingdom of God. And like in the movie, we had lots of challenges and problems to overcome as we worked to make a difference in the lives of young people.

The strategy for our staff was to find ways to interact with students at public high schools. Our goal was to serve them in some capacity, to build relationships and then to invite them to gatherings where they could hear a simple but relevant presentation of the good news. This is exactly what I had experienced as a student myself and what I had tried to do in Spokane—only now, this was my job. I was keenly aware that I was in San Francisco to learn all I could so that two years later I would be equipped to lead a work in another city.

At staff meeting one day, I found out that I was being assigned the responsibility of starting a new club at Wilson High School in the Hunters Point section of San Francisco. It was a very tough neighborhood peppered with public housing projects in the shadows of Candlestick Park, where the San Francisco Giants and the 49ers played all of their professional home games. Once I mustered up some courage, I went to the school to meet the principal and to explore how I might get involved there as a volunteer. I shared with him that I had just graduated from college and moved into the city to work for a local organization that existed to serve urban youth. I did not say much about our

Christian persuasion, as my purpose there was to find a way to serve the school.

Immediately, the principal asked me if I would be interested in coaching football. I was shocked. I thought for sure I would be assigned to police the lunchroom or to pick up garbage on the grounds, but instead they had a need for a coach, and I happened to be at the right place at the right time. I told the principal and the head varsity coach that I had played in high school, and before I knew it I was given a whistle, a gold shirt with the Wilson Knights logo, some tight, green coaches' shorts, and the responsibility of serving as the head junior varsity football coach just weeks after arriving in San Francisco. I could not believe it. Not only did I have a new job with Young Life, but I was now coaching football as a part of my ministry.

My very first day of practice, I gathered the thirty or so guys on my team to introduce myself and to figure out what kind of talent I had to work with. I was thrilled to see some huge guys on the team. The majority of the young men were either African American or Samoan—which made me very happy as a coach. The Samoan kids were all big and strong and had a reputation for being as tough as nails—great traits for football players! All of the Latino students at the school must have gone out for soccer instead. Then, to my utter surprise, hidden behind all of my gigantic players, emerged a skinny, lanky young man named Jesús, who was Mexican American. As I assigned positions to all of the guys, I asked Jesús what position he wanted to play. Without hesitation he said he wanted to play center on our offensive line, which he went on to do for the two years I served as coach.

I was so thrilled that whenever I spoke to people about my ministry in San Francisco, I was able to tell them that I was the head coach of the junior varsity football team at Wilson High School—and that Jesus was the center of my team! While everybody thought

I was being super-spiritual, I was just stating the facts: Jesús was my team's center!

I was absolutely thrilled to be surrounded by so much diversity in San Francisco. After spending four years in Spokane where I was often the only nonwhite person in the class or in the crowd, I was now surrounded by people from around the globe. The city was even more diverse than Milpitas, where I had grown up, and I loved hearing a multitude of languages being spoken everywhere I went. I was getting an education on the streets of San Francisco and was trying to figure out how my faith could be relevant in such a dynamic place. I soon discovered that the cross of Jesus had to make sense on the streets of the Mission District, not only filled with energy and vibrancy but also with violence and struggle. Two thousand years ago Jesus entered our world in a Galilean neighborhood. On the cross he embraced the pain of our world to demonstrate his love. Now, I was learning to follow his example among refugees, gays, pimps, the homeless and large Samoan football players. In the same way that God "moved into the neighborhood" in the person of Jesus, as Eugene Peterson translated John 1:14, I was now becoming fully incarnated in the streets of San Francisco. The question that began to fill my heart was, what difference did it make for God to be present in the center of my neighborhood?

During the two years I spent training in San Francisco, I continued to grow in my faith. I gave myself every day to the work of loving kids and learning about my community, and I realized how much I needed to depend on God. The fundamental practices of faith—like prayer and Scripture reading—that I began to learn about in Milpitas and Spokane were now necessary spiritual tools I counted on every day. Along the way I also learned that ministry in the city was stressful. I could sense tremendous pressure related to working with a diverse staff, handling crises with students, working long hours and learning about the fundraising challenges associated with running a Christian nonprofit organization. I felt this pressure most when I realized that I was being counted on to gain the skills that I needed to become an effective leader.

The more I was immersed in the diversity of the city, the more I began to see new expressions of racial problems and divisions. Surprisingly, I wasn't just seeing tensions in the city but was also catching wind about similar race- and culture-related issues within the mission of Young Life. As far as I could tell, these tensions were mostly due to the differences between urban and suburban ministry realities, methods and metrics of success. Although everyone in our organization had a common mission of seeing young people come to faith in Christ, there were distinct perspectives and opinions about how to reach urban kids with the gospel that were as different as night and day. Compared to the rest of the mission, much of what was happening in San Francisco was unique—and more holistic. Along with coaching football, track, wrestling and other sports, staff were leading schools clubs, teaching art, driving kids to doctors appointments, starting homework clusters and establishing a program to connect high school students and the elderly.

By contrast, much of the work of Young Life around the nation was focused and thriving in wealthy, suburban communities. In those communities it was not necessary to provide tutoring and afterschool centers, or to create jobs for students. By and large the students from these neighborhoods had all of their basic physical needs met, and what they needed most was the challenge to grow spiritually. In those circles, being faithful to gospel ministry was focused on building solid relationships with students, getting them to a weekly club gathering, establishing a "campaigner group" to help students study the Bible and get established in their faith, and attending a week at summer camp. This was the place where kids would have a dramatic encounter with the Jesus of the Bible—usually in a beautiful setting nestled among mountains, lakes, rivers and trees. Somehow, Jesus worked powerfully in these kinds of settings. For urban kids, that was a long way from the streets of the 'hood.

Living in a city with incredible needs and by many counts great animosity toward Christians, we were simply learning to be relevant as we prayed and worked for the welfare of high school students. I was not learning about the importance of incarnation from a textbook but by living in this crazy, gritty city filled with so many characters from diverse backgrounds, ethnicities and economic situations. Just two short years after moving into the Mission District, I was discovering in a very clear way the mission and burden that God was instilling in my heart—to be an agent of the kingdom in the barrios of our nation, and to do it first by incarnating my life in the neighborhood where my students and their families lived. The kind of ministry I was experiencing could not be executed by commuting into the neighborhood to serve for a few hours at a time. I was seeing firsthand the strategic importance of being present in the community 24/7—and I was beginning to understand the significance of Jesus' incarnation in a way that I had never understood before.

The summer before I was set to complete my training in San Francisco, I attended Young Life's Institute, which is designed to provide theological education for their staff. It was in a beautiful Colorado Springs boarding school we used during the summer. Staff from across the nation came to study, to connect with other staff and to be refreshed. Apparently, it was also where many staff people came to find their spouses, which is exactly what happened to me. The very first day I arrived at the summer institute in 1983, I jumped in line at the dining hall to grab some lunch. I had been in the car for close to twenty hours, driving from San Francisco with my roommate Richard, and I was definitely more exhausted than hungry. As I looked around the lunchroom to see if I recognized any of my new friends I met the year before, a very gregarious Mexican American coworker from San Francisco who had joined our staff from El Paso, Texas, ran up and gave me a huge *abrazo* (hug). Without missing a beat, he pulled me toward a very attractive young woman who was waiting in line, Marianne Nicastro. She was from Huntsville, Alabama, but was working with urban kids in Nashville. We were both extremely embarrassed by the fact that my crazy friend introduced Marianne to me as my future wife. Apparently, he was not as loco as we thought! By the end of the very short two weeks we were together in Colorado, we had a few date-like encounters—attending a movie with a group of friends, seeing each other at the library, playing tennis and meeting at a "kicker dance" at a local joint. Even so, a serious relationship seemed nowhere in sight.

After a few months of no communication, we saw each other back in Colorado at a national urban staff conference in early September. By the end of that week it was clear that our relationship was getting serious. Instead of attending a bunch of boring meetings, we spent almost every minute of that conference hanging out together.

It was at this conference that I met my good friend and mentor Luis Villareal, who was invited to be one of the keynote speakers at our gathering. He was a pastor and had served on the staff of Youth for Christ in Denver. Amazingly, Luis was the first Mexican American Christian speaker I had ever seen or heard—he inspired me with his intelligence and passion. As soon as he was done speaking one morning, I ran up to ask if we could get together for coffee or a meal. We became quick friends, and we have been walking together as *hermanos* (brothers) for the last thirty years.

I had the same kind of feelings a few years later when I heard Orlando Costas speak for the first time. This brilliant Puerto Rican theologian, who has since gone to be with the Lord, was the first Christian I had ever heard speak about the radical implications of Jesus being born as a Galilean Jew. Up to this point, in all of my studies in college and seminary no one had ever pointed out this aspect of the Jesus story.

As I began to do some research about Jesus' Galilean incarnation, I discovered the writings of a Mexican American Roman Catholic theologian from my home state of Texas, Father Virgilio Elizondo. They blew my mind. In his books *The Galilean Journey* and *The Future Is Mestizo*, he articulated the similarities between the circumstances that existed in Nazareth and the province of Galilee during the time of Jesus and the Jim Crow-like reality that existed along the US-Mexican border for Mexican Americans. Somehow, in Father Elizondo's story and theology, it became clear to me that Jesus, with his Galilean accent, entered the world to demonstrate his love to those on the margins—including kids from the barrio with struggling families, Laotian refugees striving to survive in a strange new world, and even rich, white kids trapped in deep spiritual poverty, dying to find love and meaning even while living in pristine suburban subdivisions.

Marianne and I had a whirlwind long-distance relationship with a few visits to keep us from going crazy with love. We made lots of expensive late-night phone calls before the time of unlimited cell phone minutes. Our engagement lasted just a few months. It was a crazy, fast romance capped by a very simple but beautiful wedding and reception in Nashville. My family and a few very good friends met in Kansas City, where my parents were living at the time, and they drove almost six hundred miles to Nashville in a fifteen-passenger van to join the celebration. I flew in early to see if there was anything I could do to help with the preparations before the big day, but Marianne and her friends handled all of the major details. The whole affair seemed like a dream—and when I woke up, I was a married man.

We were pretty young by today's standards when we got married, and we came from different worlds. Before Marianne met me, I'm certain she had never known a Mexican American. Before I met Marianne, I had no idea where her hometown of Huntsville was, and I was very unfamiliar with either Italian or Southern culture. But we were united in our love for Christ and in our calling to work with urban youth. Only now, Marianne was making a monumental shift from working with African American youth to becoming immersed in the mestizo world of the barrio far away from her family and from anything familiar.

Our first year of marriage in 1984 brought a ton of changes. Because of our long-distance, cross-country courtship, we had never spent more than two weeks together in the same location. Now, we were moving into a brand new city, East San Jose, that neither one of us had ever lived in before. It was a huge change for my new bride. Even though East San Jose was just miles away from where I had grown up, it seemed like worlds away. That first year of marriage we lived in a crowded apartment complex situated at the base of the San Jose foothills, with the kind of center courtyard and pool you might imagine all California properties have. Living in such close quarters with so many families proved to be cramped and noisy. We often made jokes about the variety of strange sounds that penetrated our paper-thin walls and open windows. With all of its quirks, it turned out to be the perfect place for us to start our new life together. Our long work days often ended with us eating candlelit dinners by the pool, with absolutely no privacy.

As we were adjusting to marriage, we were also getting to know our new Eastside neighborhood, which had a dozen high schools and thousands of young people who we were dying to meet. Marianne and I worked as full-time staff, and we were tasked with establishing a new urban work in this part of the city where Young Life had never ministered. We worked side by side every day with our adult fundraising committee, recruiting volunteer leaders, attending staff training functions, and praying for clarity about which high schools we would focus our ministry efforts in. It became clear to us that the intersection of King and Story Roads in the heart of East San Jose, where Overfelt High School was located, was the most strategic place to initiate our new urban youth outreach. It was in the most recognized section of the Eastside Mexican barrio known by many as Sal Sí Puedes ("Get out if you can")—only instead of trying to get out, we were praying for a way to move into the neighborhood so we could establish roots and develop relationships with folks in the community. We reasoned that if we could get a thriving ministry established at Overfelt High School, getting something started at any other school would seem easy by comparison.

Before long, we were meeting with administrators at the school, looking for ways to get involved and to meet students. I began helping with the wrestling team, which was one of the best in the state, and Marianne began substitute teaching, often having to take the assignment of subbing for the woodshop class full of rowdy Chicano teenage guys. Our goal was not only to meet the kids but to find ways to meet their parents as well. We knew we had to have their parents' trust if we were going to spend time with their children and eventually take them to camp over a hundred miles away. This was especially true of the girls, as I was fully aware that *macho* (masculine) fathers were extremely protective of their daughters. When we began to get ready for the summer, we worked as creatively as we could to get a group of guys from the neighborhood interested in attending the Woodleaf

Camp, the very same camp God used to begin to change my life just a handful of years before.

As we immediately began to look for a house to buy in the community, Young Life fortuitously established a fund to provide down payment assistance for staff looking to purchase a home, which we qualified for. Right away, we found a 900-square-foot home for sale just two blocks from Overfelt High School. Within a couple days of finding this house, which was clean, freshly painted, affordable and in a perfect location, we made an offer and became first-time homeowners.

Living in Sal Sí Puedes allowed us to see firsthand all of the interesting dimensions of life in our new adopted barrio. We were impressed by the large families, like the Perez bunch, who became fast friends and our mentors from the neighborhood. The men were hard working, and the women were even more impressive, often holding down jobs outside the home along with carrying most of the responsibilities to raise the kids, cook and care for the house. Our new neighbors shared stories about how a few years before we moved into the neighborhood, SWAT teams would jump from rooftop to rooftop chasing gang members—but they insisted things were getting better. Life on the Eastside was poorer and even more influenced by Mexican culture than where I grew up in Sunnyhills. King and Story Roads was an intersection where the lowrider car movement flourished, and it was just a block from our new home.

Every weekend, hundreds of young men and women gathered to show off their cars, tattoos and scars. This extremely visible corner of the Eastside was the place to be until the police began to crack down on the cruising, which created too much chaos and crime. Along with all of the lowriders that hung out on King and Story Roads, there was a radical group of hardcore ex-gangsters from the local Victory Outreach Church pounding the streets to preach Jesus to anyone who would dare get in their way. All of this made for amazing drama, and we had VIP seating from which to watch it all unfold. While I admired the "in your face," aggressive approach of Pastor Ed and his lieutenants at Victory Outreach, we were trying to bring a different, more relational ministry approach to the Eastside. I was convinced that a more relational way of introducing Jesus would be more effective for many of the young people in the neighborhood. I also knew that our version of faith could not be soft or watered down. We lived in a tough and extremely religious barrio, and I was learning that we had to offer something real and authentic to get a hearing, and that it might take years to do so effectively.

While I was so impressed by many of the people I met in the neighborhood, our community was plagued by crime, gang violence and low-performing schools. Too many of our young people were in jail and strung out on a synthetic drug called PCP, which was cheap and made those who used it violent—often demonstrating what many described as superhuman strength. The more I observed all of these dynamics in my barrio, the more I struggled with only attracting young people to a club meeting and getting them to camp. Instead of meeting in homes like we had in Spokane, we met with students in local parks and a recreation facility not far from the school and our home. We had to figure out how to come alongside these kids who were struggling in so many areas of their lives.

For the next couple of years, we built relationships with students. We took them to camp and attempted to draw them close to Christ. One weekend we took two busloads of our youth to Southern California to get them out of our barrio. In one crazy, long weekend, we visited Magic Mountain and Disneyland, which most of the kids had never been to before. Our volunteers spent many uncomfortable hours on the bus getting to know these amazing young people and trying to keep them out of trouble. When we arrived at Disneyland, one of my boys, Osvaldo, was pulled aside when we tried to enter the park and was not allowed entrance until he covered his multicolored Mohawk with a hat. The security officer in charge made it very clear that they would not allow anyone or anything to distract their guests from the Disney characters or attractions inside—especially not a cool Mohawk hairdo. That day at Disneyland I spent the majority of my time in the secret, underground security catacombs of the happiest place on earth dealing with some of our kids who were caught shoplifting. This was the price of working with all of these nonchurched Eastside kids, and I loved it.

Still, dealing with how to make our ministry more impactful caused me many sleepless nights. In a move that was pretty atypical for a Young Life area at that time, I made the decision (with the cautious blessing of my adult committee) to go after funding from the city of San Jose to establish a program for youth hooked on PCP, which was permeating our Latino community. I had no idea what I was doing or how to do it, but I knew we had to try to respond to the critical issues that our kids were dealing with. I was also beginning to be frustrated with the daunting challenge of helping these young people graduate from high school and get into college. Families needed to be ministered to, jobs in the community were desperately absent, our streets were unsafe, and I was beginning to doubt I had anything significant to offer the young people of our barrio that could bring relief to their daily struggles.

FOUR

Becoming an Evangelico

By the end of 1987, I felt extremely frustrated and discouraged by the lack of tangible results in our ministry. I wasn't sure how to put my finger on the key issues that were eating at me, but I had to find a different approach to working in our neighborhood. Within the Mexican American culture, being connected to the entire family was a necessity, but the majority of our relationships were in the local high school. A deeper presence in the community seemed essential. I was as committed as ever to our kids and to our barrio, but we were beginning to sense that we needed a change. Both Marianne and I felt so committed and indebted to Young Life, who had nurtured our faith and had given us our start working with youth, but we were certain that God was leading us to move beyond our ministry comfort zone. I was wondering how to incorporate the local church into our ministry efforts. I was becoming increasingly disillusioned with a proclamation-only ministry paradigm that was almost solely preoccupied with getting kids into heaven—at least, that is how I was beginning to feel. While I knew in my head that evangelism and discipleship were priorities for faithful ministry, in my heart I also had a growing sense that I could not proclaim

God's message of love with integrity without also addressing the pain and suffering of my neighbors in tangible ways. It became increasingly clear to Marianne and me that it was time for a change—it was time to leave Young Life.

I was familiar with a local organization in the city of San Jose called CityTeam Ministries, which had grown out of the local rescue mission in the downtown area. CityTeam began to aggressively expand their efforts beyond providing overnight shelter and food for the homeless by providing services to the poor and evangelistic efforts targeted at children. They established a youth outreach department led by a good friend, John Fuder, who since moved to Chicago, where he has lived for many years. The outreach spent a significant amount of energy bringing in college students from around the country and Canada to lead summer outreach programs. These summer missionaries were mostly white college students, and while they provided manpower for the work with children, the youth outreach staff had to spend a significant amount of time teaching these students how to understand the urban context and mentoring them on how to be culturally sensitive in this unfamiliar environment. CityTeam also established a camp property in the nearby Santa Cruz mountains, where each summer they took hundreds of children from some of the poorest neighborhoods in East San Jose and East Palo Alto. Just a few weeks after I resigned from Young Life, I was hired as the director of youth outreach when my friend John took on another assignment within the organization. I was not convinced that CityTeam was a perfect fit for what I ultimately felt God calling me to do, but it was time to gain new experiences in a fresh ministry setting. Going in, I was concerned that the majority of the key leaders at CityTeam were white men—a similar concern that I had experienced with Young Life. While I brought much-needed diversity to the leadership of my new ministry, a whole lot more was needed.

Up to this time in my involvement with the church, the only place I had seen Christian Mexican American leadership was in the Roman Catholic Church. When I was growing up in Texas, the parish where my abuelita would occasionally take me to mass was filled with Mexican families from the neighborhood. Unlike what I saw in the Protestant church, the priests were of Mexican descent. The church reflected the makeup of the barrio, and it was clear that the parish or local neighborhood surrounding their church facility was their ministry priority. While there was much I did not learn in my early years of attending church, I did see that Catholicism and the Mexican people were very much connected. Mexican Americans might not have been very literate and knew little about the Bible, but they knew about Jesus and his suffering. They also knew that the Virgin Mary was important to a vital faith. Huge murals of the *Morenita*—the dark-skinned Mary—were everywhere in the barrios of Texas and California, and in fact anywhere in the United States where there were Mexican Americans.

To minister effectively in the barrio, it was essential to understand the significance of the Virgin of Guadalupe. When Spanish missionaries first came to Mexico with the conquistadors, they had very little success. After nearly a generation, only a few hundred native Mexicans had converted to the Christian faith. Whether the Mexicans simply did not understand what the missionaries had to offer or they resented these people who made them slaves, Christianity was not popular among the native people.

Then in 1531 Jesus' own mother appeared to a humble Indian boy named Juan Diego. The miracles that followed convinced the people there was something to be considered in Christianity. Within a short time, six million native Mexicans were baptized as Christians.

On the morning of December 9, 1531, Juan Diego saw an apparition of a young girl at the Hill of Tepeyac, near Mexico City.

Speaking to him in the Nahuatl language, the girl asked that a church be built at that site in her honor; Juan Diego recognized the girl as the Virgin Mary. Diego told his story to the Spanish archbishop of Mexico City, Fray Juan de Zumárraga, who instructed him to return to Tepeyac Hill and ask the "lady" for a miraculous sign to prove her identity. The first sign was that the Virgin healed Juan's uncle. The Virgin told Juan Diego to gather flowers from the top of Tepeyac Hill. Although December was very late in the growing season for flowers to bloom, Juan Diego found Castilian roses, not native to Mexico, on the normally barren hilltop. The Virgin arranged these in his peasant cloak or *tilma*. When Juan Diego opened his cloak before Archbishop Zumárraga on December 12, the flowers fell to the floor, and on the fabric was the image of the Virgin of Guadalupe.[1]

No matter what critics may say of the devotion of Mexicans (and Mexican descendants) to *La Virgen de Guadalupe*, many Mexican Catholic scholars believe they owe their Christianity to her influence. It seems that when a brown Mary appeared to a lowly Indian boy and declared herself to be the mother of Jesus— the one who the Spanish missionaries were preaching—their hearts and souls were finally opened to this new expression of faith. Also the fact that Mary appeared to Juan Diego not as a European Madonna but as a beautiful Aztec princess speaking to him in his own Aztec language tied Christianity to the local people and culture in a way that had not been done.

If we want to help someone appreciate the gospel we bring, we must appreciate their culture and mentality. By understanding them we can help them to know Christ. Helping my Mexican neighbors draw close to Christ was the very thing I was determined to do.

I was grateful for a fast transition into a full-time ministry position, because by now Marianne and I had added two small boys to our family. I threw myself into my new leadership role and had much to learn about their more programmatic approach to ministry. I was also thrown into a world of suit-and-tie management. (I purchased my suits at the nearby Goodwill thrift store.) CityTeam had deep ties with the local business community, and its leadership culture was greatly shaped by many of their top leaders, white men from business and management careers and backgrounds. I was eager for the opportunity to experience a more corporate leadership environment, but my deepest burden continued to be making a difference in the poor and vulnerable neighborhoods of our city, especially in my barrio on the Eastside. The biggest challenge in my new role was to help my staff and volunteers become more relational and less programmatic, more community focused and more culturally sensitive. Instead of working in multiple neighborhoods in a very shallow manner, I convinced everyone that going deeper in a few neighborhoods would be more effective. I recruited and trained nonwhite staff and volunteers as well. We were in the heart of the largest Mexican barrio in San Jose, and I wanted our ministry to be a vibrant witness to the love of Jesus Christ, who in many ways was already ingrained into the fabric of our urban neighborhood. For the first time in my life, I started worshiping at a small church in the barrio pastored by a Mexican American leader named Fidel Sanchez. Fidel and I became quick friends and ministry partners. I was finally experiencing what it meant to be an *Evangelico*—a Latino, non-Catholic church member.

Just a year after starting at CityTeam, the director of training there, Roy Thompson, planned a training event that changed the course of my life. Roy was very excited to get all of the CityTeam staff to attend a training time with John Perkins, who I knew nothing about. Perkins told his story and began to lay out his biblical philosophy for working with the poor. John was dynamic and energetic, and in his teaching he sprinkled Bible references and stories I had never been exposed to before. Hearing John speak about Isaiah 58:12 introduced a whole new paradigm for engagement in my community.

> Your people will rebuild the ancient ruins
>   and will raise up the age-old foundations;
> you will be called Repairer of Broken Walls,
>   Restorer of Streets with Dwellings. (NIV)

The idea that as Christians we should be concerned about the physical condition of the community was a perspective that made sense to me, but I had never heard a clear biblical teaching on God's concern to see neighborhoods transformed. Ministering to individuals was front and center in my current understanding of ministry, and while the thought of meeting the practical needs of people was not a stretch for me, I was trying to wrap my head around the idea of community development as a key component of ministry. I was learning that God did not care only for people but for the communities where they lived as well.

Then John read a passage from Zechariah 8 in the Old Testament, which I had never looked at before. Again, it blew my mind because it spoke about God's desire to see unhealthy neighborhoods become healthy and vibrant places for the children and elderly residents that lived there:

> The word of the LORD Almighty came to me. This is what the LORD Almighty says: "I am very jealous for Zion; I am burning with jealousy for her."
>
> This is what the LORD says: "I will return to Zion and dwell in Jerusalem. Then Jerusalem will be called the Faithful City, and the mountain of the LORD Almighty will be called the Holy Mountain."

This is what the LORD Almighty says: "Once again men and women of ripe old age will sit in the streets of Jerusalem, each of them with cane in hand because of their age. The city streets will be filled with boys and girls playing there." (Zechariah 8:1-5 NIV)

That's what I wanted for my barrio on the Eastside of San Jose, and I was discovering that God wanted to be present in my neighborhood as well—to make our neighborhood a place where his love and peace would flourish for his glory.

The more John spoke about his work, which he referred to as Christian community development, in Mississippi and Pasadena, California, and about the power of the gospel to transform communities, the more I began to go crazy. My heart and mind were exploding with excitement as I realized that this was the kind of holistic transformation I wanted to see happen in my community, but I had no language for it. I loved that John was absolutely committed to the Bible, and that at the same time he was adamant that our faith needed to be put into action to bring about reconciliation and justice in the world. Religion was not about prosperity and emotion but about putting our energy into solving the problems of our neglected neighborhoods. This was the theological and practical ministry perspective I was dying to hear articulated, and here was this African American brother who I hardly knew giving voice to some of my deepest longings. As I listened intently to his every word, I was hearing a version of the gospel more rooted in the struggles of the poor and the oppressed. As soon as I was released from our meeting, I rushed home to talk to Marianne about everything I had heard, and to tell her about an invitation Dr. Perkins had extended to everyone at our training session to attend a gathering he was hosting in Chicago later that year.

In many ways I was going through a new conversion in my faith. In high school, as a young man desperate for the love of a father, I was converted to faith in the living God who revealed himself in Jesus Christ. Paul's words in Ephesians became real to me, and I discovered Jesus as the visible expression of the invisible God: "Christ is the visible image of the invisible God. He existed before anything was created and is supreme over all creation" (Colossians 1:15).

Until that point, faith seemed somewhat irrelevant in my life. In just a few short years, I had become a Jesus freak like my classmate in school who I thought was so weird. No question, I was a follower of Christ and was being transformed by the Holy Spirit, but I still had so many questions that needed to be answered. Now, a passionate black preacher, activist and theologian was messing up my world with his Bible teaching and his ministry philosophy, which he called the 3 Rs—reconciliation, relocation, redistribution—of Christian community development. His deep convictions about racial reconciliation, the church, community economic renewal and radical justice were resonating deeply with me. The Lord had captured my imagination through this confident yet humble man of God. John was unlike anybody I had ever met, and I was eager to spend more time with him.

After my exposure to the 3 Rs, I began to look for books and resources to expand my budding interest in the theological perspective that Dr. Perkins was presenting. I read everything he had written, but I was a bit discouraged that it was all focused on ministry in the African American community. I was longing to find a theology rooted in the Latino community that addressed the kind of issues John was surfacing for me.

My initial research led me mostly to Roman Catholic authors in Latin America. During that time, liberation theology was a vibrant movement in the Central American countries where poverty, military intervention and corruption were rampant. At the core of this theology coming from the margins was a message declaring that God gave preferential attention to those on the periphery of society. God came to offer liberation, not primarily from personal sin but from unjust economic, political or social conditions—which were also expressions of sin. The term *liberation theology* was first used in 1971 by a Peruvian priest named Gustavo Gutiérrez, who wrote the book *A Theology of Liberation*, which began to fuel a movement that spread to Brazil, El Salvador, Uruguay and beyond. Father Oscar Romero, a Catholic priest in El Salvador who was martyred for standing with the poor, became a hero in the struggle for justice in that region. But a major criticism of this theology was its connection to Marxism.

In a region of the world filled with so much injustice, a call to action for believers of the most radical leader in history, Jesus Christ, resonated greatly. Instead of focusing on themes championed in the West, and specifically in the US church—personal piety, holiness and the need for people to be saved from their individual moral sins—liberation theology was calling out unjust systems, governments and economic policies that created war and intense suffering. A great divide existed between these two worlds. Those reading the Bible from a perspective of wealth and white privilege were leery of political involvement of any kind. Those situated among the poor believed political engagement to bring about justice was absolutely necessary for change in their communities and nations. I had to figure out how to reconcile the radical understanding of faith and liberation, which I was learning from these authors, with my faithfulness to the theology that was strongly influencing my life and my ministry coming out of Young Life. I latched on to John Perkins's teaching as an anchor for my new theological explorations.

October 1989 arrived before I knew it, and I was thrilled that

Leo Charon, one of the big dogs at CityTeam, and I were assigned to attend the conference John Perkins spoke about. I had only been to Chicago once for a few days to attend a Seminary Consortium for Urban Pastoral Education (SCUPE) conference, which was a lot like our Christian community development conference is today. Once in Chicago, Leo and I took the train from the airport to Oak Park where we were staying, and then made our way to the African American neighborhood of North Lawndale, where the conference was being held. We shyly stepped off the "L" platform and exited the rundown station onto the main drag that ran through this rough urban neighborhood. After getting our bearings we began looking for Lawndale Community Church. We mistakenly entered an old whitestone church building just blocks away from our destination, and were directed to the church gym down the street. When we arrived, we were greeted by members standing in front of the church, which once was an old Cadillac dealership. Rumor had it that the notorious Al Capone once bought his cars here. The building was later purchased by the Salvation Army before Lawndale Community Church was finally able to acquire it. As we arrived, we met leaders from around the nation with their own stories about how they ended up at this meeting.

The common denominator for everyone there seemed to be an encounter with John Perkins. Apparently, we had all been inspired by John's teaching of the 3 Rs, and by his ability to make everyone feel as if they were his best friend. During the next two days, we listened to some stirring and brutally transparent presentations by Bob Lupton, from Atlanta, and by Mary Nelson, who worked in a nearby Chicago neighborhood and had the same kind of bent and passion that I had heard in San Jose from Dr. Perkins. We also sat through meetings designed to obtain consensus on the birthing of a national association with the purpose of bringing together leaders from around the nation committed to restoring marginalized neighborhoods. It was during these meetings that I first met the young, baby-faced white pastor of Lawndale Community Church. Everybody called him "Coach," and he would soon be appointed the president of this new association. I was keenly aware that the majority of the leaders at this meeting were focused on ministry in the African American community. Thankfully, a Puerto Rican brother named Elizar Pagan and I were there to remind folks about the need to include Latino communities in our discussions. Elizar was elected to the founding board of our new association.

For my coworker Leo, this meeting was inspiring and interesting. For me, our time at this small church in one of the poorest and most rundown neighborhoods I had ever seen was revolutionary. My impression was that this African American church led by this young, white pastor from Iowa was still a bit fragile, but it was exactly the kind of community-based church ministry I imagined was needed in East San Jose. I loved that there was a full-size basketball court alongside the meeting room where Sunday worship was held. I loved that a young doctor had just established a health center to meet the medical needs of the neighborhood. I absolutely loved that youth ministry was such a strong priority. And I loved that the leaders of Lawndale Community Church were a mix of black and white believers living and serving together in this urban community. Everything that Dr. Perkins talked about was coming to life in this unique church environment. While I was excited to be present at the founding of CCDA, I was even more exhilarated by what I was seeing modeled by this church and its members.

The night before I was set to leave Chicago, a few of us jumped into the car of a woman from the church, who drove us a few blocks south to a Chinese restaurant in the adjoining neighborhood. Ironically, we were in one of the largest Mexican barrios in the entire Midwest, and instead of eating *carne asada* (grilled meat) at *Nuevo Leon,* a corner restaurant filled with locals, we were eating Chinese food! However, I noticed that everyone on 26th Street or *Avenida Mexico* was of Mexican descent, and that all of the business signs throughout the neighborhood were in Spanish, with the exception of a Radio Shack. As I walked around the block to take a closer look at this barrio, it reminded me more of a large border city like Tijuana or Nogales than a neighborhood on the west side of Chicago. I could not help but get excited about the possibility of living and doing ministry in a place like this. That evening, I called my wife and told her that I had discovered a Mexican neighborhood called La Villita smack in the middle of Chicago. This bustling urban community, with cold weather and long winters, was an unlikely place for Mexican immigrants to settle. But at the end of the Bracero Program, which literally means "manual labor," it became a landing point for immigrants from south of the border, and now for a new wave of Mexican immigrants coming to the United States to find work.

The Bracero Program was initially prompted by a demand for manual labor during World War II and began with the US government bringing in a few hundred experienced Mexican agricultural laborers to the Stockton, California, area. The program soon spread to cover most of the United States and provided workers for the agricultural labor market (except for Texas, which initially opted out of the program for an "open border" policy). Simultaneously, the railroad Bracero Program was independently negotiated to supply US railroads with much-needed, unskilled workers to provide maintenance for the expanding railroad tracks. Eventually, *braceros* (migrant workers) were utilized to provide other types of unskilled labor. By 1945, the quota for these programs was more than 75,000 braceros working in the railroad industry and 50,000 working in US agriculture at any one time.

The growth of Mexican labor in the United States that resulted from the Bracero Program came under increasing criticism and resulted in the deportation of over one million Mexican workers in 1954 in an effort called Operation Wetback. There was increasing concern that Mexicans were taking jobs from Americanos, as well as concern over increasing abuse of the braceros living and working in America. The Bracero Program was officially ended by Congress in 1964, but not before over 500,000 Mexicans were allowed to enter our country to work legally through this program. By now, our nation was becoming dependent on the cheap labor of Mexican workers. Many of these braceros stayed in the United States, and many settled in Chicago's Westside, in neighborhoods like Pilsen and Little Village. While many Mexicans stayed in our country without legal status, the government mostly turned a blind eye to this situation because of our continued need for cheap Mexican labor.

Even though these workers were needed for their cheap labor, they suffered great discrimination. In Texas, where I was born, the same kind of discrimination that we associate with African Americans in this country was experienced by Mexicans, who had to endure "White Only" bathrooms and lunch counters, as well as deplorable living and working conditions. In Chicago, Mexicans were mostly tolerated and often treated as human buffers between whites and African Americans fighting to carve out their distinctive neighborhoods. By 1989, there were over one million Latinos, mostly of Mexican descent, in the Chicagoland area, and 100,000 of them lived in La Villita.

Marianne could hear the excitement in my voice, and I was so encouraged as we began entertaining the possibility that a move to Chicago might be something we should consider. While we loved our Eastside neighborhood in San Jose, a drastic change of venue like this might be just the opportunity we needed to put into practice all that we had been learning about community development. After seeing firsthand what Coach referred to as the "Lawndale Miracle" because of all of the ways that God answered prayers as the church began, I could imagine starting a similar community church in the vibrant barrio that had just come on my radar. Another factor that made this wild idea a real possibility was the fact that Marianne's family would be just a ten-hour drive from Chicago, instead of across the country. A burden from God had been planted in our hearts.

Not long after I returned home to my family and to my demanding responsibilities at work, Marianne and I were convinced that the Lord was calling us to make the cross-country move to the Windy City with our two young sons, Noel Luis and Stefan. A few days after Christmas, and just a couple of months after I was eating noodles in La Villita, Marianne and I made a trip to Chicago to meet with Coach and to spend some time in this barrio that had captured our hearts. The city was experiencing an arctic blast unlike anything we had to endure in sunny California, and we were thankful that Coach kept his appointment to meet with us at his office on that freezing December morning. We spent about two hours together and drilled him with a million questions about Chicago and his knowledge of La Villita. While he seemed supportive of our enthusiasm to relocate to Chicago, and offered to help us if we came, he was very honest about what it would require of us to establish a bona fide community development ministry. At the very least, he said, we should plan on making a fifteen-year commitment or not bother coming at all. This audacious challenge got our attention, but it did not derail our growing sense that we should move to the barrio of La Villita.

Two massive barriers keep the US church from doing ministry among the poor: (1) our wealth and privilege, which isolates us from the poor, and (2) our inability to persevere when ministry results don't come quickly. From our perspective of Western privilege, our theology and understanding of ministry lack connection to those on the margins. Almost all of my classes at Whitworth, and even at Fuller Seminary through the partnership they had with Young Life, were taught exclusively relying on German and other dominant-culture theologians. The classical theologies I had to study were rooted in a perspective of power. While this training served me well to a certain extent, I'm not sure it adequately prepared me for church ministry among the poor. Themes like suffering and perseverance were surely touched on as we studied the passion of Jesus, but as soon as we left class we moved into our comfortable accommodations far removed from the poor.

Two new insights were percolating in my heart that would be central to the development of our new ministry in Chicago:

- I was serving a God who puts the margins at the center of his concern, not only to bring about individual transformation but justice as well.

- Living in my new barrio would help me to discover what happens when God is at the center of a neighborhood.

In late January 1990, I resigned from CityTeam and prepared to leave for Chicago with no job and no income in sight. Subsequently, I took a job with a good friend, Jon Singley, who owned a landscaping company. For the next few months I worked alongside a mostly Mexican crew mowing lawns and digging ditches to feed my family—a bit humbling! At the same time we began the process of raising funds for our new ministry. We got some tremendous support from my brother-in-law Norm and from a few close friends who loved and believed in us. In record time, we miraculously raised the finances we needed to pursue our new vision in Chicago. By the time summer arrived, I found myself crossing the Midwest in a U-Haul truck with the help of my dad and my brother, heading to our new home in the largest Mexican community in the Midwestern United States.

Marianne and the boys flew from California to Alabama, where I would pick them up after I stuffed all of our belongings into a storage unit. I had made a special trip to Chicago in the middle of summer to look for a home to purchase, with no success. In the end, we reluctantly decided to rent an apartment on the border of Oak Park and Austin, a couple of miles from La Villita, until we could locate a permanent place to call home. Along with commuting into La Villita almost every day to begin the work of meeting people and finding a house, I also started to take a seminary class downtown that afforded me the opportunity to ride the "L" and get familiar with this amazing urban metropolis. A few weeks later, we found a small, single-family brick house that needed a total rehab job on the western edge of our neighborhood. Our only hesitation about moving into this section of our neighborhood was the fact that our realtor called it the "Gold Coast" of La Villita— which we quickly came to discover was more than a slight exaggeration. We bought and totally overhauled this old house, and finally moved into our barrio in December 1990, a few months after arriving in Chicago. We were ready to start developing our new ministry in this amazing Mexican community, and there was no other place we wanted to be.

A decade after initiating our ministry in La Villita, I was invited to speak at a Moody Bible Institute pastors' conference in Chicago. My assignment was to provide these pastors with a biblical framework for understanding our work in poor communities. Of course, my presentation would have to be rooted in Scripture.

My hope that day was to help these pastors gain a better understanding of what a holistic, nontruncated expression of the good news looks like when it is lived out in the center of a vulnerable neighborhood by men and women seeking to be good neighbors. It was in this context that I first presented the key concepts that I write about in this book. My premise then was the same as it is today: In order to effectively minister in a vulnerable neighborhood in a way that is truly biblical, our ministry has to include the following components of ministry: incarnation, proclamation and formation, demonstration of compassion, restoration and development, and the confrontation of injustice.

At the center of my framework is the most familiar and important symbol of our Christian faith—the cross. On the scandalous cross of Golgotha, our Galilean Savior takes the sins of the entire world upon himself to liberate all of humanity from our alienation from our heavenly Father and from other imperfect human beings. He not only sets us free from the penalty of death but also from a life of hatred, envy, racism and indifference to the suffering of others. He sets us free to become champions of *justicia* (justice) in our broken world.

Having received such a great salvation, we can be no longer content to perpetuate or preach a one-dimensional gospel that is only concerned about securing people's immigration status in heaven as redeemed citizens of the kingdom. Now, we go into the world as agents of the kingdom of God that Jesus initiated when he entered our human reality. Our prayer now is "Thy kingdom come, Thy will be done in earth, as it is in heaven" (Matthew 6:9-10 KJV). In a very real sense, this is where the cross meets the street—in places and neighborhoods where we encounter the very people that Jesus came to love and liberate: in the streets of the barrio, the ghetto and the most vulnerable neighborhoods of our nation.

FIVE

Incarnation

Just weeks after moving into the neighborhood, I walked two blocks behind
our home to visit the local elementary school. I knew that if I made
myself available, as I had in San Francisco and San Jose, there would
be opportunities to serve. After talking to Principal Dominguez for
just a short while, I was approved to tutor a group of fifth grade
students in reading. Later in the week, he called me into his office
and gave me another assignment—to take all of the eighth grade
students sentenced to detention and create a project with them to
keep them out of trouble. I came up with the idea of helping the
kids design and paint murals in the hallways of the school. My
project was approved with one small change—our murals would
have to be painted in the grimy boys and girls bathrooms on the
main floor. Spending hours with these kids in the bathrooms was
no easy task, but it gave me great credibility with everyone at the
school because no one could believe I was willing to invest my time
with these difficult students on a project like that. By the start of
summer, we were able to invite to a summer program and Bible
camp many of the children and youth I got to know at the school.
Because we lived so close to the school, this and many other opportunities to serve and get to know our neighbors came our way.

Long before I had ever heard of John Perkins or had ever read the Chinese poem he often quotes (see sidebar) to start a conversation about the philosophy of Christian community development, I instinctively knew that living in the neighborhood where I was called to minister was the best way to get to know those I felt called to love. I had no choice about living in Sunnyhills with my family. But when I arrived in San Francisco I was thrilled to be living in a vibrant urban community that put me in contact on a daily basis with so many of my neighbors. In Sal Sí Puedes, being a homeowner down the street from the school where we were ministering made it convenient to hang out and meet kids. The fact that all of the students lived in our barrio made it possible for us to really understand their concerns and dreams.

> Go to the people
> Live among them
> Love them
> Listen to them
> Learn from them
> Start with what they know
> Build on what they have
> And, of the best leaders
> When their work is done
> The people will say
> We have done it ourselves
>
> **Lao-Tzu**

Now that we were living in La Villita, we began to meet our neighbors and got to know as much about our neighborhood as possible. Our new barrio was a wonderful place to call home. Nearly one thousand thriving businesses and *taquerias* (taco shops) lined 26th Street; there were several fantastic parks, and friendly faces were always willing to offer a passing *"Buenos dias"* (good morning). But we soon discovered that La Villita was also riddled with difficulties. We had more than our share of unemployment and crime, as well as the dubious honor of having the Cook County Jail located in our barrio. Additionally, we discovered that a large percentage of the immigrant population in our community was undocumented, so poverty and employment issues were an ever-present challenge. In short, we could not imagine a better place in the United States to work out what it means to be an agent of God's kingdom.

By now I was also paying more attention to the theological and missiological importance of our being present in our neighborhood. Realizing that I was following the example of Jesus himself, who left heaven to enter our world, gave me great encouragement and even greater resolve to lean into the day-to-day realities of our new neighborhood. I reasoned that if we were going to have an impact in this community for the kingdom, it would begin by simply being present. John 1:14 became a foundational text to help me better understand the importance of living in the community.

> So the Word became human and made his home among us. He was full of unfailing love and faithfulness. And we have seen his glory, the glory of the Father's one and only Son. (John 1:14)

Beyond solely focusing on the theological significance of God entering our hurting and decaying world en carne in the person of Jesus of Nazareth to rescue and restore all of creation, I found a powerful example of how to enter into the lives of those I was being called to love. When I read this verse in *The Message* version of the Bible that "The Word became flesh and blood and moved into the neighborhood," I marveled at the reality that the neighborhood of Jesus' day was very similar to the barrio of La Villita I had moved into.

Reading authors like Virgilio Elizondo, Samuel Escobar, René Padilla, Viv Grigg, Justo González, Orlando Costas and John Perkins helped me to see that God revealed himself on the margins of human existence, and it absolutely revolutionized my understanding of God's character and of the priority of the poor in his redemptive plan.

When people began to suspect that Jesus might be a prophet or the Messiah, they often asked whether anything good could come from Nazareth. At the beginning of his public ministry, even his disciples had a hard time wrapping their heads around the idea that the Messiah that Moses prophesied would come from a despised and unexpected place like Nazareth.

The following day John was again standing with two of his disciples. As Jesus walked by, John looked at him and declared, "Look! There is the Lamb of God!" When John's two disciples heard this, they followed Jesus.

Jesus looked around and saw them following. "What do you want?" he asked them.

They replied, "Rabbi" (which means "Teacher"), "where are you staying?"

"Come and see," he said. It was about four o'clock in the afternoon when they went with him to the place where he was staying, and they remained with him the rest of the day.

Andrew, Simon Peter's brother, was one of these men who heard what John said and then followed Jesus. Andrew went to find his brother, Simon, and told him, "We have found the Messiah" (which means "Christ").

Then Andrew brought Simon to meet Jesus. Looking intently at Simon, Jesus said, "Your name is Simon, son of John—but you will be called Cephas" (which means "Peter").

The next day Jesus decided to go to Galilee. He found Philip and said to him, "Come, follow me." Philip was from Bethsaida, Andrew and Peter's hometown.

Philip went to look for Nathanael and told him, "We have found the very person Moses and the prophets wrote about! His name is Jesus, the son of Joseph from Nazareth."

"Nazareth!" exclaimed Nathanael. "Can anything good come from Nazareth?"

"Come and see for yourself," Philip replied. (John 1:35-46)

Shockingly, Jesus entered the world in a social reality more closely resembling the barrio, with all of its issues, than it did the pristine and secure suburbs we value so much in our North American culture. Nazareth, which was located in Galilee, is where Jesus spent the majority of his time preaching, healing and ministering. It was becoming clear to me that Jesus not only came into the world to preach good news to the poor (Luke 4:18), but that he actually became poor himself to identify with those on the margins of society. Sean Freyne observes,

> Given the importance of Jerusalem to Jewish thinking at that time, I wondered why Galilee had become such an important point of reference in the Gospels. Galilee seemed of little or no importance in the Hebrew Bible, and apparently had negative connotations for some of the people (Matthew 21:10-11; John 1:46, 49; 7:52). It seems to me that Galilee must have been of special salvific significance to the first Christians, since it plays an important role in the post-Easter memory of the followers of Jesus and became part of the earliest kerygma (Acts 10:37-41). The question pressed itself: Why is Jesus' ethnic identity as a Jewish Galilean from Nazareth an important dimension of the incarnation, and what does it disclose about the beauty and originality of Jesus' liberating life message?[1]

The fact that our God-turned-Galilean entered a social and political reality rooted among the poor and culturally marginalized of his day caused me to reexamine the theological significance of this aspect of the incarnation. It was shocking that Jesus entered the world in a marginalized community in Galilee, which was seen as a region full of sinners because of its mix of Gentile cultures, diverse languages and religious beliefs that constantly called into question their authenticity and purity as Jews.

Commenting on the disciples' denial of Jesus to the Roman officers, Orlando Costas used to say, "Peter could deny Jesus three times, but the moment he opened his mouth to talk, he could not deny that he was a Galilean, because of his distinctive accent."[2] Jesus spoke with that same distinct Galilean accent!

Because so much of my own Christian formation had been developed in the context of our dominant Western culture, with its limited theological perspective, I had never been challenged to consider the ramifications of this amazing historical reality—Jesus was considered to be culturally suspect because of his Galilean upbringing. He was looked down upon by the dominant Jewish culture because of the way he spoke and because of the side of the tracks he lived on—experiences very common for the millions of Mexican Americans and other ethnic minorities in our own society.

I was beginning to read and understand the story of Jesus from the margins of the barrio, and I was overwhelmed by the realization that Jesus launched his kingdom ministry to the entire world with a ragtag team of Galilean men and women from a mestizo and marginalized reality. While I was tempted to conclude that Jesus was part Mexican, I was more certain than ever that he was not the white version I had always pictured in my mind. To be understood, Jesus had to be seen in his historical and cultural reality as a Galilean Jew. In that

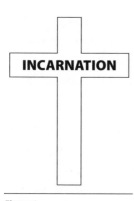

Figure 1

context, it was unmistakable that Jesus of Nazareth identified with the marginalized, the oppressed and the vulnerable—and I was determined to do the same in my ministry.

In effect, I was beginning to see incarnation as the linchpin and foundation for all effective ministry—by entering people's lives through proximity, relationship, solidarity and humility, I would be following the example of Jesus himself (see fig. 1).

PROXIMITY

When my two boys were still young, I was offered the opportunity to be the chaplain for the Chicago Cubs. Although it was a clear deviation from my primary burden and call to work with the poor and marginalized, I agreed to serve in this role. Not only would it be a change from my everyday ministry, but it would also be exciting for my boys who loved baseball. Through my connection to a ministry called Baseball Chapel, I was assigned the responsibility of offering a chapel service for the Cubs players every Sunday before their home games, and to do the same for the visiting team. As a baseball fan and a follower of Christ, this was an exciting time.

In order to effectively minister to the guys on the team and to their wives and girlfriends, I had to spend as much time as I could at the ballpark to get close to the players. After getting my season pass, which allowed me to attend all of the home games, and being assigned a parking spot directly next to Wrigley Field, I was ecstatic. At the end of my first season, I was given permission by the front office and the manager to travel to away games with the team, to stay at the Ritz-Carlton where the players stayed, to fly on the team's chartered plane, and to enter the clubhouse with almost total liberty. Even though I could never totally enter the lives of these professional baseball players, if I was going to effectively reach them for Jesus, I had to do everything possible to get as close to guys like Joe Girardi and Sammy Sosa as I could. If being in close proximity to these ballplayers was necessary to help me be more effective as an agent of God's love, how much more would it be necessary in my work with the residents of La Villita.

Living in close proximity to those we are called to minister to, regardless of the context, makes all the difference in the world! Can you imagine if God had taken a safer and less costly approach to bringing about salvation? Can you imagine Jesus commuting to Nazareth from heaven every day instead of being fully present in the everyday situations of his family and neighbors? Yes, proximity made all the difference in the world for Jesus, and it would be the key to establishing an authentic presence among my neighbors.

RELATIONSHIPS

A woman in the crowd had suffered for twelve years with constant bleeding, and she could find no cure. Coming up behind Jesus, she touched the fringe of his robe. Immediately, the bleeding stopped.

"Who touched me?" Jesus asked.

Everyone denied it, and Peter said, "Master, this whole crowd is pressing up against you."

But Jesus said, "Someone deliberately touched me, for I felt healing power go out from me." When the woman realized that she could not stay hidden, she began to tremble and fell to her knees in front of him. The whole crowd heard her explain why she had touched him and that she had been immediately healed. (Luke 8:43-47)

In the Gospels, Jesus had the unique ability to make everyone feel loved and important, and that was the foundation of his influence on those around him. Moving from seeing our neighbors as targets of ministry to seeing them as friends begins with establishing relationships. Once these relationships deepen, we earn the right to speak into people's lives, and we gain the credibility to share our stories in a way that touches people's hearts and souls. It is also through these relationships that *we* are transformed, because relationships are never a one-way street.

Along with volunteering at our local school, I explored ways to get connected to the health center that Lawndale Community Church had established to serve the medical needs of the underserved community. Because of the clinic's proximity to La Villita, many Spanish-speaking patients were showing up there to get their medical care. Eventually, the decision was made to serve our large Mexican population just south of North Lawndale's primarily African American population. This necessitated hiring some bilingual staff. An exceptionally talented young woman, Irene, who eventually attended our church, became the key Spanish-speaking person at the clinic, and she often introduced me to patients from La Villita.

Late one afternoon I got a call from Irene and one of the doctors asking if I would visit the home of a family who was going through a crisis. The wife and mother of this family came to the clinic seeking help for her alcoholic husband, who was on another drinking binge. He was sprawled on the floor of their home, and she did not know what to do. I got the address and made one of my first pastoral visits to meet this family who lived just blocks from our home.

Somehow, I was able to get Manuel sobered up, and I began to spend many hours with him, his wife and his children. Over the years, Juanita and the kids began to get very involved in our ministry and eventually became strong believers, but it all began with the establishment of a relationship with her husband, who never got strongly connected to our church. Manuel taught me a great deal about the struggles of the men in the community and about the pressures they felt having to endure long workdays, low-paying jobs and very little respect. In many ways, getting to know men like Manuel helped me to understand my own father, who had to endure many similar experiences. I would take every opportunity I could to spend time with Manuel and his family, and to engage him in my world as well. One day, Manuel and his *tocayo* (person with same name) Manuel Lopez, who he had met at an AA meeting, helped me put a new roof on my garage. While getting the job done, I realized the shingles were noticeably crooked. I also realized that my two *amigos* (friends) were hung over while helping me lay my new roof.

Jesus made everyone he encountered feel loved and important, whether it was the leper who nobody else would touch or the woman who had been bleeding for years that no one would listen to. Jesus demonstrated a willingness to get involved and to build relationships with people just where they were. If I could find ways to do the same thing, I was sure we could make a difference in our neighborhood.

SOLIDARITY

The first Easter I spent in La Villita, I saw up-close my Mexican American neighbor's powerful identification with the suffering of Jesus, especially on the cross. Every one of the eight Catholic parishes in our barrio were filled with men, women and children eager to commemorate the passion of the cross with a fervor that I had never experienced before. The reenactment of the *Via Dolorosa* ("Way of Suffering"), which takes place in every Mexican barrio on Good Friday, was vibrant, dramatic and a vital expression of faith to my neighbors. At a place like Whitworth College, very far removed from the suffering of the margins, my study of the redemptive work of Christ seemed to emphasize Jesus' suffering "for" us as something that had very little to do with our lives today. Here, the fact that Jesus was willing to suffer "with" us, as a suffering servant while he redeemed us, was quite powerful. Unlike the exclusive focus on the resurrection that most middle-class evangelicals tend to emphasize, a strong connection and preoccupation with the suffering of Christ was clearly seen as a significant element of God's redemptive intervention. Somehow, on the cross, Jesus not only offered redemption and forgiveness for our sins, but he also demonstrated absolute solidarity with every man, woman and child who had ever experienced extreme suffering, rejection and humiliation. "This High Priest of ours understands our weaknesses, for he faced all of the same testings we do, yet he did not sin" (Hebrews 4:15).

My longtime mentor and friend Father Virgilio Elizondo, who has given his life to minister at the San Fernando Cathedral in San Antonio, in a barrio also called La Villita, provides this insight regarding the significance of Jesus' willingness to enter into the suffering of humanity and how that connects to the daily reality of the Mexican American people:

> Some persons working with Mexican Americans have thought it would be better to shift the emphasis from the cross to the resurrection. I would agree if the situation were changing in such a way that we could say that resurrection was indeed becoming a meaningful symbol. But this is not yet the case.[3]

One of the huge challenges we faced as parents when we moved into the neighborhood was the same concern that every parent in our barrio had about gang violence and the safety for our small kids. As our boys got older and were ready to start school, we were also extremely concerned about the quality of the schools they would be attending. After a great deal of turmoil, prayer and conversations with friends and school administrators, we were very fortunate to get our oldest son, Noel Luis, admitted to a fabulous public magnet school outside of our neighborhood. The school was technically open to all of the kids in our city, but we struggled immensely with the decision not to send him to the local school where I had begun to volunteer close to our home. We were committed to living in solidarity with our neighbors, yet we found ourselves ready to send our son to a much better school than most of the other kids on our block. The fact that these magnet schools were very difficult to get into made it even more difficult to not take advantage of the opportunity.

We realized that even though we lived in the neighborhood and were committed to being there for the long haul, living in full solidarity with our neighbors was not always going to be possible. The fact that less than 5 percent of our barrio's residents had a college degree gave us a huge advantage educationally. The sobering reality that we always had the option and ability to leave if things got too hard meant that there were limits to our ability to fully enter into the world of our neighbors—even though I am Mexican American myself. Being honest about this was extremely humbling and sobering. In our efforts to live in solidarity with our neighbors in La Villita, we became keenly aware of our own limitations. We realized we were not prepared to sacrifice our children's education because of our calling to live in the neighborhood.

HUMILITY

> You must have the same attitude that Christ Jesus had.
> > Though he was God,
> > > he did not think of equality with God
> > > as something to cling to.

Instead, he gave up his divine privileges;
    he took the humble position of a slave
    and was born as a human being.
When he appeared in human form,
    he humbled himself in obedience to God
    and died a criminal's death on a cross. (Philippians
    2:5-8)

One of the most embarrassing obstacles I had to overcome when I became the pastor of La Villita Community Church was my inability to speak or read Spanish fluently. Regrettably, my siblings and I, like many of the second- and third-generation Mexican American youth in our neighborhood, had become accustomed to speaking to my parents in English, even when they spoke to us in Spanish. By the time I graduated from high school, I spoke almost zero Spanish!

When I arrived in La Villita, I was intimidated because so many of the residents in our community spoke Spanish as their primary language. If I was going to have any significant ministry here, I would have to get over all of my inhibitions and begin to practice my Spanish, even though I knew I was going to butcher the pronunciation of many words. The idea that love covers a multitude of sins often came to mind, because I had to depend on the love and patience of my brothers and sisters at church to help me relearn my first language.

People in our church were very gracious to me—yet every time I spoke Spanish was an adventure. The very first sermon I preached in Spanish was on Easter Sunday, 1991. I was so nervous that I wrote my entire sermon in both English and Spanish so I could read it as easily and correctly as possible. Toward the end of my sermon I emphasized that when the disciples examined the tomb where Jesus' body was laid, they saw that the tomb was *vacío*—empty. I mispronounced vacío by leaving out the accent, and I had no idea what I had done. After the service, one of my leaders gently informed me of my mistake, and I was not only humbled but also humiliated!

In a strange way, God used my struggle to relearn to speak Spanish fluently to allow my immigrant and mostly uneducated neighbors to be my teachers. I actually needed my neighbors to help me learn to communicate effectively, a bit like Moses needed Aaron's help to speak to the crowds. I'm sure this is part of the reason that Moses describes himself as the humblest man on earth. So I was in good company. Instead of seeing myself as the "Great Brown Hope" coming in to save everyone, as I often fancied myself to be, I had to humbly accept my limitations and go about the work of bettering my Spanish one day at a time.

My Mexican neighbors are often described as being very humble and respectful people. Many of them work as cooks, janitors, factory workers, dishwashers and maids, and it is not an uncommon experience for them to be looked down upon by others simply because of the kind of work they do and because of their ethnicity. When I listened to the stories about their work experiences, I remembered walks I took with my grandfather when we visited Mexico. He would take me by the hand and tell me in Spanish, *"Ten cuidado con los bolillos, porque te van abusar"* (Be careful with those Anglos, because they are going to abuse you). That was his experience working as a janitor at the local high school, and unfortunately that was the experience of many of my church members and neighbors in their workplaces as well. In order to treat my neighbors with respect and dignity, I had to understand this aspect of their lives—and I had to empty myself of the temptation to see myself as superior in any way.

Nothing helped me avoid paternalism and condescension toward my neighbors more than living and worshiping with them on a regular basis. As we all came to the cross of Jesus, equally broken and in need of forgiveness, we were united in our humanity as well as in our brotherhood and sisterhood in Christ. It was even more imperative for our Anglo church members and leaders to find ways to relate to our Mexican neighbors as equals. We were learning together that the kind of humility we needed to practice had more to do with consistently making decisions to give up power and share leadership. More than being meek, quiet and mild mannered, we all had to work at treating each other with respect, and we needed to humbly look for ways to serve one another. Honestly, this was more difficult than we imagined.

Whenever I traveled to speak about our work in La Villita, I often met young men and women excited about the possibility of moving into our barrio. I found it critical to emphasize that if they came, it had to be with a posture and attitude of humility, and they had to be willing to serve under the leadership of men and women from the community. I feared that instead of coming into the neighborhood to learn, listen and simply get to know and love their new neighbors, they would move into our community wanting to fix and save everyone they met. I had to keep watch to assure that we all avoided this trap.

For many, the idea that we were willing to incarnate our lives into our Mexican barrio seemed radical, but we were simply following the pattern of Jesus when he entered into his Galilean neighborhood over two thousand years ago.

SIX

Proclamation and Formation

Therefore, go and make disciples of all the nations,
baptizing them in the name of the Father and the Son
and the Holy Spirit. Teach these new disciples to obey all
the commands I have given you. And be sure of this:
I am with you always, even to the end of the age.

Matthew 28:19-20

My phone alarm woke me at 4 a.m. so I could get ready for my upcoming speaking trip to a respected seminary. I was prepared and excited to present three talks, but I was sad to be leaving home again after a one-night stop between trips. I had just returned home from a fantastic trip to Buffalo, New York, where I had the privilege of speaking at one of our CCDA member churches located in a tough neighborhood on the edge of a housing project. The church was launched six years ago by a leader groomed in a large suburban church; his heart was gripped with a burden to establish a vibrant church body in the inner city. Not long after making this move, this pastor of this church attended our national CCDA conference, and he began to intentionally shape his ministry around the philosophy of Christian community development.

During that trip, I presented my cross diagram various times. It was the subject of my teaching at their Sunday morning worship. I presented it again during an evening Q&A session with leaders from around the city of Buffalo. Finally, I drew my cross diagram on a napkin at a local coffee shop for the senior pastor of the large suburban church that had supported the planting of the ministry I was visiting. Although I had shared this message hundreds of times in the past year, I was just as excited to present it again, because I am convinced that it is the kind of biblical framework that Christ-followers need to grasp and understand if they are going to effectively engage in ministry in vulnerable neighborhoods.

Now, I was headed to an academic setting on the other side of the country to present the same message. Instead of helping grassroots leaders and pastors, I was going to speak to hundreds of theology students who were inundated weekly with theologically challenging messages. It was my hope to expand their paradigm of kingdom ministry. I began my talk by quoting Matthew 4:23-25 about the good news of the kingdom:

> Jesus traveled throughout the region of Galilee, teaching in the synagogues and announcing the Good News about the Kingdom. And he healed every kind of disease and illness. News about him spread as far as Syria, and people soon began bringing to him all who were sick. And whatever their sickness or disease, or if they were demon possessed or epileptic or paralyzed—he healed them all. Large crowds followed him wherever he went—people from Galilee, the Ten Towns, Jerusalem, from all over Judea, and from east of the Jordan River.

After reading these verses, I asked the students an important question. Is there a difference between what American Christians think is the good news and what Jesus taught regarding the good news of the kingdom?

I then drew a diagram on a whiteboard that I had been taught in seminary and in some of my discipleship classes (see fig. 2). It was presented as a clear and simple way to understand and share the gospel, the good news, with others:

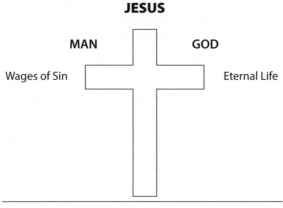

Figure 2

In this classic diagram, I was taught that the death of Jesus on the cross was the bridge between sinful human beings and the perfect God. By confessing our personal sin and putting our faith in Jesus, we would be saved from the wages of sin and hell, and receive the promise of eternal life. This diagram was a simple way to communicate the good news—and sharing this with as many people as possible seemed to be the ultimate expression of faithfulness to God. After all, this was the core message of our faith. "For God so loved the world that he gave his one and only Son, that whoever believes in him shall not perish but have eternal life" (John 3:16 NIV).

While I was in total agreement with the basic premise of this diagram, I pressed the students to consider that this understanding of the good news was woefully incomplete without a strong and vital connection to an incarnational approach to evangelism and discipleship. Simply getting the message out in a way that targeted as many people as possible without personal connection or relational interaction was not the ideal, especially not in the 'hood! To be biblical, proclamation and formation had to be tied to incarnation (see fig. 3). My experiences in La Villita only verified this conviction.

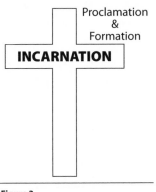

Figure 3

I was emotionally, physically and spiritually exhausted by the end of the long counseling session I had with Jose Luis and Herminia. This couple had come to Chicago from Puebla, Mexico, years earlier to find work and a better life for their family. Jose Luis was a line cook, and Herminia was a housewife who also held down a few odd jobs. Their income often ran out each month before their expenses were paid, and their financial troubles often caused tremendous tension at home. A few years later I found out that this family was fortunate to have their immigration green cards, which gave them permission to work legally—although they could not vote and were not yet citizens. Still, making ends meet was almost impossible, and raising three kids on their salary would be a stretch for anyone. More significant than their money problems were their marriage problems. Their relationship was on the brink of destruction. The more time I spent with them, the less optimism I had for their crumbling marriage.

Watching this marriage fall apart was brutally painful, and I struggled with being able to offer this couple any meaningful counsel or encouragement. Instead, when I met with them, my mind would often race back to the struggles that my mom and dad had in their marriage. What I remembered most vividly was the empty and void look in my mother's eyes—as if she were numb from years of sorrow. Emotionally, my mom had learned to survive like a cactus in the desert, with dangerously low levels of love, affection or affirmation. I could see that same look in Herminia's eyes, and it made me crazy angry. I desperately wanted to have compassion for her husband, but it was very evident that his heavy drinking, rage and extreme jealousy were destroying their marriage.

Through the love and prayers of countless leaders in our church, we began to see changes in this couple's relationship. They began to attend a Bible study and started showing up with their three children for our Sunday service. Our long hours of conversation and counseling began to bear fruit, and before I knew it, the love of Christ had begun to push away the pain and anger from their hearts and replaced it with his grace and forgiveness.

This is why we had made the cross-country move from sunny California to the tundra of Chicago—to see peoples lives transformed and to provide a church that would nourish their faith smack in the middle of the barrio! I knew that God could change lives if we were faithful to do our part. I had seen the change in my life. After so many discouraging years, I eventually saw it in my family as well. My mother came to faith in Christ like most of us do, out of desperation, and God met her with the kind of tender embrace that she was dying to experience. With the floodgates of God's love opened and released in my family, my two sisters and brother also came to faith in Jesus. Penetrating my dad's macho, armored heart would not be as easy, but God was clearly at work in his life as well. A new relationship with Jesus was transforming my family, and I knew that it could do the same for families in La Villita.

Our arrival in La Villita to establish a church and a community ministry began to attract others with a similar vision. Dan Swanson had recently returned from living in Mexico, where he worked in a church, and was excited to connect with our new work. Mike and Terry Kijowski, an eye doctor and a nurse, were working at the Lawndale Clinic, and they moved into the neighborhood to join our efforts. Rick and Lara Starrett, also doctors at the clinic, had a passion for the Mexican people and came onboard. Irene Moreno, from Venezuela, somehow found us and became a key leader in our ministry. Dan Phipps, a contractor, connected with us and later with Irene, and they eventually got married. After moving into La Villita without knowing a soul, a mission team was beginning to form.

Within months of arriving in Chicago, I received a call from a student at Moody Bible Institute asking for a meeting. The next day I was sitting with this young *tigere* (ladies' man) from the Dominican Republic and New York talking about theology, church and life. Robert was strong and direct, and had a passion for evangelism. Unlike many of the Mexican American leaders I knew who tended to be more understated and reserved, he came at me with strong opinions and bold visions.

Robert had been going through a transformation in his own theological development. In one of his classes, he wrote a paper on the growth of liberation theology in Latin America, capped off by watching the movie about the life and assassination of Archbishop Oscar Romero. We became fast friends as we began to meet regularly to get to know each other and talk about our emerging church in La Villita. His eyes would light up when we talked about unbelievers he was building relationships with. They would light up even more when we started talking about the church and theology. From those first meetings, it was easy to see that I was the community activist and Robert was the teacher and theologian. We would spend hours lamenting the state of American evangelical churches, who we concluded had zero passion for the proclamation and sharing of the good news. We both agreed that the formation of Christ-followers through intense discipleship was a lost art as well. We shared our own faith journeys and how strong, committed Christians had invested their lives to disciple us; we wanted to do the same thing for others. We were tired of seeing the Great Commission inscribed on walls and lit up on huge Jumbotrons for all to see, without seeing evidence that Matthew 28 was being lived out by the members of these churches.

The more Robert and I prayed and strategized about how to work together, the more it became clear that he and a small group of his classmates from Moody should put on hold their initial plans to start a new Spanish-speaking church somewhere in Chicago and join our efforts in La Villita. I was overwhelmed with excitement. I knew that we needed a strong Latino, Spanish-speaking leader on our team, and Robert would be a perfect complement to my leadership. The fact that he was not Mexican was only a small issue for me. As it turned out, while Robert was totally ready for this change, the move proved to be a paradigm shift for the other students involved. As they prayerfully considered the possibility of relocating into La Villita, they never imagined that they would be refocusing their evangelistic efforts in one specific barrio.

I began to meet with our core leaders and repeatedly reminded them of the importance of helping our neighbors come to faith in Christ from within the context of incarnation, as we had seen enough examples of drive-by "shock-n-awe" evangelism, which often did more damage than good. We had seen too many large suburban churches target our urban barrios and poor ghettos from their suburban outposts in an effort to get as many of our people saved as possible. They had good intentions, but not the best approach. We wanted the growth of our church to come from within the community, and we had no desire to be a commuter church. The majority of the non-Roman Catholic congregations in our barrio already seemed to be commuter churches, with very few of their members actually living in the vicinity, and we were determined to be different.

I was convinced that if we loved the men, women and children in our barrio, we would have an opportunity to communicate God's love in a compelling and respectful way. Because so many of our neighbors already considered themselves Catholics, our goal was not to take people from their churches. Instead, our goal was to help our neighbors get connected to Christ and to encourage them in their spiritual growth. If we did that faithfully, we were pretty certain that many of them would eventually get integrated into our church familia. Increasingly, millions of Latinos from both the United States and Latin America were becoming evangelicos— seen especially in the dramatic growth of Spanish-speaking Pentecostal churches throughout the world.

The story in Luke 5 that describes how Simon left everything behind to follow Jesus was a constant inspiration to me as I worked to build relationships in La Villita.

> One day as Jesus was preaching on the shore of the Sea of Galilee, great crowds pressed in on him to listen to the word of God. He noticed two empty boats at the water's edge, for the fishermen had left them and were washing their nets. Stepping into one of the boats, Jesus asked Simon, its owner, to push it out into the water. So he sat in the boat and taught the crowds from there.
>
> When he had finished speaking, he said to Simon, "Now go out where it is deeper, and let down your nets to catch some fish."

"Master," Simon replied, "we worked hard all last night and didn't catch a thing. But if you say so, I'll let the nets down again." And this time their nets were so full of fish they began to tear! A shout for help brought their partners in the other boat, and soon both boats were filled with fish and on the verge of sinking.

When Simon Peter realized what had happened, he fell to his knees before Jesus and said, "Oh, Lord, please leave me—I'm too much of a sinner to be around you." For he was awestruck by the number of fish they had caught, as were the others with him. His partners, James and John, the sons of Zebedee, were also amazed.

Jesus replied to Simon, "Don't be afraid! From now on you'll be fishing for people!" And as soon as they landed, they left everything and followed Jesus. (Luke 5:1-11)

When we encounter Jesus in this passage, we find him at the Sea of Galilee, where some scholars believe he might have worked as a carpenter before he left everything to begin his public ministry. He had probably eaten his lunch by the waterfront as he built homes that were springing up in this region for the wealthy Roman officials that vacationed along the Galilean shores. He knew that the shore would be filled with fishermen and with locals ready to purchase fish for their families. Like Jesus often did, when he was determined to engage in someone's life, he jumped right in. This day, he jumped into Simon's empty boat. From there, he taught the crowds with his wisdom and insight into his Father's love.

When he was finished speaking, he asked Simon to launch the boat into deeper water and to cast out his net. At first, Simon pushed back, maybe in frustration, as he explained to Jesus that he and his crew had worked all night without catching anything. The idea of trying again so soon was not in his plans. Still, Simon listened to Jesus and cast out his nets, not expecting any results. What happened next was miraculous. When Simon began to pull up his nets, there was such a huge catch that the net began to break. The boat was filled with fish and was on the verge of sinking!

In awe, and not knowing what else to do, Simon Peter fell to his knees and began to ask Jesus for forgiveness for doubting him, and because he knew he was not worthy to be in the same boat with Jesus, who was showing himself to be God. Peter and his partners were awestruck with their catch, and also with Jesus, who had intervened in their lives and blessed them. Now, he told the fishermen to stop being afraid and cautious; Jesus had even bigger plans for their lives, which included making a difference in the lives of people. Captivated by Jesus' love and power and his bold vision to see people's lives transformed, they dropped their nets, left everything behind and followed Jesus. Had Peter known that he would eventually become the leader of the church, he might have thought twice about getting out of that boat.

If we were going to see a change in our barrio, it would begin with inviting our neighbors to get to know the love and power of Jesus, and to begin to follow him as Peter, James and John had done on that lakeshore many years before.

A brother by the name of Bob Salinas, who was a pocho like me, began to introduce me to many of the young men in the community who were involved in gangs. We desperately wanted a place where we could gather these kids to keep them out of trouble. The gang violence in our community was severe, and with my youth worker background I was determined to get our church involved in working with these youth. By now we had moved out of the daycare space we rented for worship and on Sunday mornings rented a large, four-story building in the heart of the neighborhood. The arrangement we had with Arturo, the building manager, was shaky at best. Another church in the neighborhood had bought the building but was not currently using it. As they waited to determine how they might utilize this great space for their own ministry, they allowed Arturo to manage their building.

Every weekend, Arturo rented the large hall that we used for our worship space to be used for dances, *quinceañeras* (celebrations), weddings and parties, which of course included drinking until the wee hours of the morning. Early on Sunday mornings I, and anyone else I could guilt into coming, would clean, scrub, disinfect and deodorize the entire building in preparation for our worship service, Sunday school and fellowship time. We dreaded the weekly ritual of trying to eliminate the smell of urine and alcohol that permeated the entire building. The place was old and the bathrooms were in terrible shape, but we could not find a better place to meet. We not only wanted a place to worship, but we also needed a place to work with these young men that Bob was introducing us to, and we could not utilize the building during the week. Eventually, with the help of the Lawndale ministries, we were able to buy this building, which expanded our ability to serve the children and youth of our community. This bold step also created the challenge of owning a huge building in need of major repairs.

We were fully committed to developing the men, women and youth of the community into strong, committed and spiritually mature leaders, but it was not an easy task. I was beginning to see that whenever committed and mission-minded individuals from outside of our community relocated in our barrio and got involved in our small but growing body, the more our Mexican brothers and sisters would step back and defer to the leadership of these relocators, especially the empowered white doctors and teachers we were beginning to attract. Our goal was to empower and cultivate leaders indigenous to La Villita, but in many ways, we seemed to be working against this goal.

Not long after starting a formal Bible study with some of the adults and a summer program for the children we were getting to know, I got a call from the US director of International Teams, who was living in North Lawndale and was investing his life at Westlawn Gospel Chapel along with a great team of African American leaders. Mark had begun to recruit missionaries who would be willing to relocate into urban neighborhoods instead of going overseas. After some intense and lengthy conversations about their strategy, I was impressed that Mark and his team seemed committed to having their missionaries take a very low-profile, humble posture in the ministries where they were assigned. Even though I was not crazy about the term *missionary* because of so many negative connotations it evoked, I really liked Mark and was impressed with his heart.

I agreed to have three white individuals from IT join our church-planting efforts. The young couple and single woman immediately moved into La Villita and were available to serve under our leadership in any way we desired. This was a great blessing because we had no staff and no money. The fact that they raised their own support seemed too good to be true.

I never expected that what seemed to be such a positive arrangement would end up having such unintended consequences. As I listened to the men and women in our church speak about our new missionaries, I suspected we might have a problem. Along with members of our church offering incredible praise for these three, I heard women comment that they could never be as spiritual as these wonderful leaders, who spent all of their time praying, visiting people at their homes and studying the Bible. Our folks often worked ten-hour-per-day jobs and came home to impossible responsibilities. They could not see themselves measuring up to the educated, professional, missionary Christians who were now leaders in our church. None of us had bad intentions, but we were in danger of stifling the growth and development of some of our most committed community leaders we wanted to raise up.

I felt a tremendous tension as a leader and as a pastor, because I desperately wanted to see our church grow. Robert and I were full of vision. Some incredibly gifted leaders had joined our team, but we were trying to do too much too fast. In those early days I was in a hurry to do everything that our ministry was supposed to do. I was impatient, still very immature as a leader and determined to build a successful church. I tried to lean on the wisdom and support of Coach Gordon and Lawndale Community Church, who were our formal partners, but I was destined to learn by trial and error. Pastoring a church that was so culturally and economically diverse tested every ounce of my leadership ability, and I was often coming up short.

About this time my parents returned to California after living in Kansas City for about a decade. General Motors had gone through some restructuring at the Fremont plant where my father had worked in the Bay Area, and he had been given the choice of relocating or losing his job. He did what needed to be done and endured the cold and snow of the Midwest until it was time to retire back home to California. Instead of returning to Milpitas, where my parents had lived for years, they sold our childhood home to my sister Veronica and her husband Manny and moved to Modesto, California, about one hundred miles east of Milpitas in the Central Valley of California. Here they found a slower-paced life and a more affordable place to call home.

After being in Chicago for a number of years, I spoke to my old Young Life friends about the possibility of my speaking at their Woodleaf Camp during the month of August. Although I was no longer on staff, they agreed, and I was able to take my family, now with the addition of little Anna, to experience camp for an entire month. I was thrilled to have them spend time in the place that God used to change my life. Like a good Mexican, I invited my parents and all of my siblings to come and spend a week with us at camp. My parents ended up coming for a week. It would be a great time for them to see their grandkids, and my mom and dad would get a chance to see me in action, proclaiming the good news to hundreds of mostly unchurched youth.

It was a special week, and on the last day before my parents were ready to head home, Dad attended the club time, as he had all week. Day by day, I presented the story of Jesus's coming en carne to give us new life, and how he sacrificed his life for the cleansing of our sins. It turns out, it wasn't just the kids who were paying attention. After the club time my father found me in my cabin and asked if we could talk. He went on to say, "How can anyone hear the story of God's love that you have talked about this week and not respond?" It seemed that after so many years of resisting the Lord in spite of our prays and pleas, Anselmo was ready to surrender his life to Christ. Tears flowed for both of us, but I was somewhat skeptical. Even though Jesus had offered him forgiveness, I was still not sure I was ready to absolve my father of his sins!

My family and I returned home to Chicago refreshed and energized. We had a growing nucleus of men and women committed to our ministry and to our barrio. We had big dreams to make a difference for God's kingdom. We were fully committed to staying rooted in the community long term. We were confident that our efforts to evangelize and disciple our neighbors in La Villita would bear much fruit.

SEVEN

Demonstration of Compassion

Pure and genuine religion in the sight of God the Father
means caring for orphans and widows in their distress
and refusing to let the world corrupt you.
James 1:27

After Marianne and I decided we were ready to move to Chicago, we began to speak to as many friends and family members as we could to share our vision and to begin raising the funds we would need to start our ministry. We had no denomination backing us, so we had to depend on the generosity of our friends who believed in us to get us started. I was willing to get a job once I arrived in Chicago, doing whatever was necessary, but the ideal scenario seemed to be having three years of support raised before we arrived. This way, we could focus on building relationships and figuring out our ministry plan.

Immediately, a group of friends committed to helping us. We were in a couples group for many years, with some amazing men and women, and they came alongside our efforts wholeheartedly. But no one helped us quite like Marianne's brother, Norm

Nicastro. Norm had been a Young Life staff person for close to twenty years, and he was so excited for our new adventure that it seemed like he was moving to Chicago with us. With his help, and with the support of many of his good friends who also knew Marianne, we miraculously reached our fundraising goal and arrived in La Villita with our salary and a small ministry expense budget pledged for three whole years. This was an amazing blessing! One night we were in Huntsville, Alabama, at a fundraising dinner Norm had put together with some friends. At the end of our presentation, a woman told us she was amazed that we would be living on a family income of under $25,000 per year. That was in 1990, so to us, it was a lot of money. We assured her that we could do it, and she promised to pray for us.

When we arrived in La Villita and saw the extremely meager economic situations that many of our neighbors had to endure, we realized that we were rich in comparison. And because we sold a home in California, we came to Chicago with enough equity to purchase and rehab a very nice house, and only one family lived in our huge three-bedroom house! It was not unusual for two or three families to live together until they each could afford their own apartments or homes.

Now that we were living in the midst of what seemed to be such overwhelming need, I was constantly reminded of two of Jesus' most powerful and poignant teachings related to being compassionate toward those in need: the good Samaritan teaching in Luke 10 and the end times teaching of the sheep and the goats in Matthew 25.

Let's look first at the parable of the good Samaritan:

> Jesus replied with a story: "A Jewish man was traveling from Jerusalem down to Jericho, and he was attacked by bandits. They stripped him of his clothes, beat him up,

and left him half dead beside the road.

"By chance a priest came along. But when he saw the man lying there, he crossed to the other side of the road and passed him by. A Temple assistant walked over and looked at him lying there, but he also passed by on the other side.

"Then a despised Samaritan came along, and when he saw the man, he felt compassion for him. Going over to him, the Samaritan soothed his wounds with olive oil and wine and bandaged them. Then he put the man on his own donkey and took him to an inn, where he took care of him. The next day he handed the innkeeper two silver coins, telling him, 'Take care of this man. If his bill runs higher than this, I'll pay you the next time I'm here.'

"Now which of these three would you say was a neighbor to the man who was attacked by bandits?" Jesus asked.

The man replied, "The one who showed him mercy."

Then Jesus said, "Yes, now go and do the same." (Luke 10:30-37)

The story of the good Samaritan is a great challenge to me. Almost every day I encounter people in need as I leave my home to walk or drive to the "L" station or to my office, which is just a few blocks away. It is not unusual for me to urge folks to avoid walking from our house to the Central Park station late at night because of the potential dangers along this main drag that connects our Mexican and African American communities. Dangerous journeys on the streets of Chicago, which is one of the most violent cities in the nation, are a common reality for those who live here.

Not too long ago I was rushing out of my house to get to my office with a full day of ministry activity scheduled in my calendar. Just as I stepped into my car, I noticed that there was a body lying on the grass on the side of my home, which is on a corner lot. Seeing strange things along the side of my house is not unusual. As I took a closer look, I could see that it was a young man covered in blood; he looked like he might be dead. I cautiously walked toward his lifeless body and tried to shake him awake without any success. By the look of the tattoos on his body and the way he was dressed, I surmised that he was a local gang member from our community. Already late for a meeting, I was not anxious to get involved. I felt guilty about leaving him there to die, especially if one of my neighbors was watching me. Finally, more out of guilt than wanting to be a good Samaritan, I called 911. While I was making the call, a fire truck pulled up with alarms blaring. It turns out that one of our neighbors had been watching this whole thing unfold, and she called for emergency help right away. I had no idea if she was a Christian, but I know her actions were much more Christlike than the way I had reacted to the situation. To make things even more exciting, as soon as the fire truck arrived, the man jumped up to his feet, pulled up his pants that were almost falling off his body and ran off as fast as he could. We were all standing in shock at what we had just seen.

In Luke 10, Jesus tells a story of a man who had been beaten up and left to die on the dangerous road to Jericho. A priest and a worship leader walked past this hurting man, but instead of stopping to help they crossed to the other side of the road to avoid having to deal with the situation. Next comes a Samaritan, whose people were despised by the Jews because of their cultural impurity and unorthodox faith. In Jesus' story, this Samaritan man, and not the religious leaders, who should have known better, took the time to help the helpless man. The story tells us that the Samaritan put the man on his own donkey and took him to get help. After tending to his wounds, he left the man to recuperate with an innkeeper and promised to cover all his expenses.

After telling this dramatic story, Jesus asked a very important question. "Which one of these three was a neighbor to the man who had been attacked by bandits?" The expert in the law who asked Jesus the initial question responded, "The one who showed him mercy."

Jesus famously told him to go and do likewise. Being men and women of compassion in our needy world and risking involvement, even to the point of being inconvenienced, is a clear way to love our neighbor. Jesus made it clear that regardless of our orthodox theology, our consistent church attendance or even our full-time ministry vocation, loving our neighbor requires the demonstration of compassion as a regular practice of our faith (see fig. 4). By making an intentional decision to live in a vulnerable neighborhood, we are almost guaranteeing that we are going to encounter needy people on a regular basis.

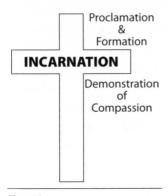

Figure 4

In Matthew 25 Jesus teaches us that love and action toward the most vulnerable in our world is intimately connected to himself. Jesus does not only care for the poor and call us to do the same, but in a mysterious way he is also actually present in the poor.

THE FINAL JUDGMENT

But when the Son of Man comes in his glory, and all the angels with him, then he will sit upon his glorious throne. All the nations will be gathered in his presence, and he will separate the people as a shepherd separates the sheep from the goats. He will place the sheep at his right hand and the goats at his left.

Then the King will say to those on his right, "Come, you who are blessed by my Father, inherit the Kingdom prepared for you from the creation of the world. For I was hungry, and you fed me. I was thirsty, and you gave me a drink. I was a stranger, and you invited me into your home. I was naked, and you gave me clothing. I was sick, and you cared for me. I was in prison, and you visited me."

Then these righteous ones will reply, "Lord, when did we ever see you hungry and feed you? Or thirsty and give you something to drink? Or a stranger and show you hospitality? Or naked and give you clothing? When did we ever see you sick or in prison and visit you?"

And the King will say, "I tell you the truth, when you did it to one of the least of these my brothers and sisters, you were doing it to me!"

Then the King will turn to those on the left and say, "Away with you, you cursed ones, into the eternal fire prepared for the devil and his demons. For I was hungry, and you didn't feed me. I was thirsty, and you didn't give me a drink. I was a stranger, and you didn't invite me into your home. I was naked, and you didn't give me clothing. I was sick and in prison, and you didn't visit me."

Then they will reply, "Lord, when did we ever see you hungry or thirsty or a stranger or naked or sick or in prison, and not help you?"

And he will answer, "I tell you the truth, when you refused to help the least of these my brothers and sisters, you were refusing to help me."

And they will go away into eternal punishment, but the righteous will go into eternal life. (Matthew 25:31-46)

Both of these clear and powerful stories push me to recalibrate my understanding of true faith as having the poor and the vulnerable at the center of my concern. I could not escape the fact that at every turn in the Gospels, Jesus was conversing with someone who was suffering, needy, sick, dying or enduring some kind of oppression. I was becoming more convinced that my response to individuals who were in need revealed more about my understanding of God's love and compassion than any degree or lofty ministry plan I might have.

With so much need in our world, I wonder how so many of us in the West who claim to be followers of Jesus—this Jesus who was always hanging around the needy and the distressed—could be so isolated and detached from the poor. How could our own nation, with such staggering wealth, be home to millions of men, women and children living in extreme poverty? How could the poorest and most neglected neighborhoods in our country exist in the shadows of unimaginable abundance and opulence? And why are the majority of the poor in our country people of color?

The tension to know how to help our friends and neighbors in La Villita was complex. Unlike tourists who were visiting downtown Chicago and being approached by anonymous homeless people, I was constantly being confronted by the needs of people I was getting to know up close and personal. Almost every day I would get a call from someone asking for help with an electric bill or rent. Being in the middle of our immigrant community with 100,000 residents and immense needs meant that the problems never seemed to end. When I was confronted with a need, I would always ask as many questions as I could, trying to discern if and how I could intervene. More often than not, I felt frustrated and overwhelmed.

Once the word got out that La Villita Community Church was a place where people cared, we had more opportunities to help others than we could handle. I was most devastated when I encountered single mothers working tirelessly to raise their kids. I could not imagine how some of the Mexican women I met could make it on their own in a place like Chicago. The difficulty of trying to survive, often so far away from home and family, was unimaginable to me, but survive they did.

There was one particular family, a mom and three sisters, who began attending our church. All of them were without husbands, and the sisters each had children. Each shared a tragic story of how she was abandoned by her man. Somehow they arrived in our barrio hundreds of miles north of the US-Mexican border. While I was thrilled to see them involved in a women's Bible study and attending our Sunday worship, I became very concerned to see how dependent they were becoming on the financial support of our members. We dealt with crisis after crisis, and their situation did not seem to be stabilizing. It was excruciating, but we had reached the limit of emergency aid we could offer them. After many conversations, I finally offered to make them a small loan they could use to establish a business selling *elotes* (corn) and *frutas* (fruit) on 26th Street. The money we loaned them as a church would be used to purchase a wheeled cart they could use to sell their food. We were committed to supporting this family, but we had to find a different way to help. It took a few years, but they eventually repaid that loan.

As we established our ministry, we did not have the wisdom found in Bob Lupton's book *Toxic Charity* to help us maneuver the land mines associated with providing appropriate expressions of compassion. In his book, Lupton shows how well-intentioned people are actually hurting the very people they're trying to help. The poor end up feeling judged, looked down upon and worthy only of charity and handouts, making them more dependent instead of learning skills to help themselves. Churches and charitable organizations, though well-intentioned, have missed the mark when it comes to serving the poor, creating a toxic form of charity. A better system would be to treat the poor as business partners, empowering them to start businesses, build houses, plan communities and ultimately take control of their own lives with the support of compassionate, caring believers.

Our goal was to create opportunities for our neighbors to become empowered so that they could provide for themselves and for their families and not to create dependency. We saw the devastating effects that welfare and poorly conceived programs offered by the government and churches had had on entire communities, and we were determined to stay away from that kind of approach. Instead of lifting people out of poverty, we knew that it was possible to hurt them instead by offering charity in an inappropriate manner.

In my travels I visited a food pantry that had just completed a major renovation of their facility. It was a beautiful place to pass out food. At the end of the tour of this awesome facility, the director shared with me that there were families in their program who they had been helping for over twenty years. When I heard that, I asked if they were concerned about keeping people dependent on their program year after year. It turned out to be a very awkward moment.

We were learning that compassion without incarnation could be devastating.

Without being present with the people we were trying to empower on a regular basis, it was impossible to know if our attempts to intervene were appropriate or not. Outside-in efforts of compassion could ultimately create more problems for the people of the community—especially the children. Whenever I had conversations with friends who had gone on missions trips into Mexico or other places around the world, they would agree that this dynamic was a consistent problem.

Across the border in Juarez, Mexico, I found one of the most extreme examples of creating dependency I had ever seen. After decades of sending thousands of kids on missions trips into the barrios of Juarez, on the other side of El Paso, it seemed that every neighborhood along the border was peppered with missionary church outposts developed to accommodate the yearly visits of youth groups from across America. Flying the flags of every denomination imaginable, these groups would carry in Bibles, building materials and clothes, and come prepared to invade their designated barrios with the preaching of God's Word—usually through a translator. In one particular barrio of less than thirty thousand residents, over fifty such US-supported mission efforts were established. These churches invested thousands of dollars and hours of service to the poor in the name of Jesus.

Unfortunately, when the drug violence began to escalate along the border, all of these outside partners and church groups disappeared. The parents of young people in places like Alabama, Oklahoma and North Carolina became horrified at the thought of allowing their children to continue going into such dangerous situations. These groups stopped coming, and slowly, almost every one of those fifty churches ceased to exist without the outside support they were once receiving.

On a recent visit to Juarez, I met Pastor Antonio Briones, who was still open for God's business in this community. He had been the pastor of a large Methodist church for more affluent Mexicans in another section of the city, and by his own admission they had very little concern for the poor. He pastored a growing church of over 2,500 members and was enjoying the success of his ministry. This all changed when he was mistakenly kidnapped to be killed by a drug lord. As he was waiting to be shot by his captors, this pastor began to examine his life and fading passion for Christ. (I guess being kidnapped causes one to do that.) Miraculously, toward the end of his ordeal, someone came storming in to where he was being held and ordered him to be released. They discovered they had kidnapped the wrong person!

After finding his way back home, he left his church pastorate and was determined to realign his life to serve the poor he had neglected for so long. He and his family bought a piece of property on a sandy lot in the barrio of Anapra, just a stone's throw away from El Paso, and established a school for the children of the community. He was convinced that the greatest need that existed in this community was not another church that might disappear tomorrow, but a place to empower the children and eventually the community as well.

GLEANING IN LEVITICUS

In our own situation in Chicago, I was grateful that our church was connected to a movement like CCDA, which was teaching us to focus on empowerment instead of creating dependency. The biblical principles that we were being taught by Coach Gordon and John Perkins emphasized the need for people to work and to take responsibility for their lives and their futures. We knew that we had to find ways to apply the gleaning principle that was found in Leviticus 19:9-10: "When you reap the harvest of your land, do not reap to the very edges of your field or gather the gleanings of your harvest. Do not go over your vineyard a second time or pick up the grapes that have fallen. Leave them for the poor and the foreigner. I am the LORD your God" (NIV).

As I reflected on this text, I knew that God was calling us to care for the poor in our barrio, but he was instructing us to do it in a way that allowed the needy to work and maintain their God-given dignity. Making people stand in line to receive free food and clothing was to be avoided. When men and women went to the clinic to see a doctor, they had to pay a minimal fee if they had no insurance. If they could not afford the fee, they could wash windows or do some cleaning in exchange for their medical care. No one was so poor that they could not contribute something.

When we began our afterschool program, we knew that parents needed to invest something in this ministry that was serving their kids. If they could simply drop off their children for hours without any investment, they would eventually feel entitled to our support. When we found out that some parents were having a hard time coming up with the small fees we were charging, we asked them to come in and volunteer to cook, clean and help tutor the other children in our program. By providing a chance for the moms and dads to participate and invest in their children's development, everybody won.

FEEDING THE FIVE THOUSAND

We knew that many of the parents in our community had little or no formal education, and so meeting with teachers and even with our afterschool staff was very intimidating for them. Some of the parents could not read or write in Spanish, let alone in English. But these were bright and intelligent men and women who had so much to contribute, and when we encouraged them to get involved and serve, what they could do was amazing.

It was very similar to the approach of Jesus who was mobbed by thousands of spiritually starving men and women eager to hear him teach about the kingdom of God (Matthew 14). As evening grew near, over five thousand men, women and children were still hanging on his every word, and now they were not only starving for spiritual nourishment but for food as well. Jesus miraculously fed the entire crowd with only five loaves of bread and two pieces of fish—barely enough food for a small boy's lunch. Instead of raising his hands and zapping food into people's laps, Jesus acknowledged his heavenly Father as the provider of every good gift in prayer and then proceeded to ask his disciples to distribute this Happy Meal to the hungry masses. I wish I could have seen the look on Peter's face as he took those tiny pieces of fish and bread into his humongous hands and began passing them out to the crowds. Finally, he was using his fishing skills for the kingdom.

This is exactly what we needed to do to empower our people. We had to believe in them. We had to let them fail and make mistakes. Yes, we had to stick to our mission of raising up leaders from the community. Compassion would not be the end goal but the gateway to individual and community development.

JESUS HEALS A MAN WITH LEPROSY

> In one of the villages, Jesus met a man with an advanced case of leprosy. When the man saw Jesus, he bowed with his face to the ground, begging to be healed. "Lord," he said, "if you are willing, you can heal me and make me clean."
>
> Jesus reached out and touched him. "I am willing," he said. "Be healed!" And instantly the leprosy disappeared. (Luke 5:12-13)

Another vital principle in combating paternalistic approaches to one-way charity, which causes so much damage, is the importance of personal touch. In the same way that Jesus reached out his hand and physically touched the man who was suffering from leprosy, we worked hard to do the same thing with our neighbors. Everywhere we looked, the poor were treated as objects and numbers, not as valuable human beings. When a poor person went to the public aid office or was forced to go to a free clinic, she or he often became a faceless number waiting to be helped. Like the leper in Dr. Luke's account who was considered unclean and thus isolated from the community, his family and even the temple, the poor from our barrio, especially the undocumented, were often *maltratados* (mistreated). They were made to feel repulsive, offensive and subhuman.

In a startling move of compassion, Jesus ignores the religious and cultural mores of his day by making physical contact with this man and thus risks being considered spiritually unclean. Not only was the man cleansed of his leprosy, but he was also transformed by the personal touch of a human being—Jesus of Nazareth—who as a Galilean Jew understood perfectly well what it felt like to be looked down upon and rejected. No wonder the crowds were so attracted to Jesus!

CONCLUSION

To have compassion toward humans is not to pity them for their misfortune or situation, but to acknowledge the connection we have to their pain. It means coming alongside them to temporarily ease their pain and suffering in a manner that does not take away their dignity, knowing that one day they may do the same for us.

When compassion reaches its limits of usefulness, we must take a different tactic. We must begin the work of restoration and development.

EIGHT

Restoration
and Development

About ten miles north of La Villita is the real Gold Coast of Chicago. It is lined with mansions big enough to fill a *pueblito* (small town) full of people. The quaint streets are picturesque and sparkling clean, and just a five-minute stroll from Michigan Avenue's Magnificent Mile that plays host to Gucci, Prada, Ralph Lauren, Hugo Boss and the Trump Tower. Along with the thousands of extremely wealthy residents who call this stretch of real estate home, millions of visitors from around the world are drawn to this chic outdoor street/mall to shop till they drop.

Less than a mile west of all of this glitz and glitter was Cabrini Green, which was once home to one of the most infamous public housing projects in the nation. Unless you saw Cabrini Green in its heyday, it was hard to imagine. Not long after arriving in Chicago, I was befriended by Bill Leslie, one of the city's urban ministry pioneers. Bill was the founding pastor of La Salle Street Church, which was sandwiched between the Gold Coast and these projects, and Bill spent the best part of his life working to bridge the gap between these two worlds. By the time I got to know Bill, he was no longer the pastor at La Salle but was then investing his time mentoring younger leaders like myself. Before Bill died of a heart attack, we met in a small accountability group for about eight years. Before his passing, he witnessed the beginning stages of gentrification in Cabrini Green that converted one of the most dangerous and notorious gang-infested neighborhoods in the city into the most controversial urban housing redevelopment in the entire nation.

Cabrini Green was located too close to the Gold Coast and to the beautiful lakefront of our spectacular city to not be targeted for urban renewal. The land was too valuable to continue housing the poor in their dilapidated high-rises, and much too desirable to be wasted on families who lived off the government. It was time for a change. The neighborhood needed to be safer and more attractive. Being so close to the Magnificent Mile, it was time to attract more businesses and to bring back the gentry who had left the city years ago because of violence and urban decay. It was time to reclaim this part of the city for the thousands of ex-suburbanites entering this new urban frontier with gusto and preapproved mortgages. The fact that this large-scale invasion of townhomes and luxury condominiums was displacing scores of mostly African American residents who had lived there for decades was not their concern. These new pioneers were simply taking advantage of a market opportunity to live in one of the greatest city centers on the planet. Gentrification with justice was not on their minds.

In contrast, in La Villita we were facing many issues as a community, but gentrification was not one of them. Our schools were overcrowded, our homes were filled to the brim with expanding families, and unlike Cabrini Green we were too far from downtown for any kind of development by the city. Even though our immigrant community contributed more sales-tax revenue to Mayor Daley's coffers than any other business community except for the Magnificent Mile, we were mostly ignored and safe from any outside development plans.

AN ANCIENT CITY IN RUINS

Jerusalem was in ruins, but God used a man named Nehemiah to spearhead one of the most amazing urban renewal projects in history. In spite of the amazing work that he accomplished, very few Christ-followers know much about his life or his work. In fact, almost every teaching or commentary I have been exposed to about Nehemiah has focused exclusively on general leadership principles or has been related to a church capital campaign. Usually, a local pastor will preach from this book to remind his congregation that just as Nehemiah and his people were able to rebuild the walls of Jerusalem in fifty-two days, they too can complete their building project on schedule and without any debt.

I discovered, though, that the book of Nehemiah is actually about the strategic importance of rebuilding and restoring a city in ruins. In the final period of Jewish history recorded in the Old Testament, we find this account of how the son of exiled Jews working in the Persian government uses his position, skills, political influence, connections and dynamic faith to restore the walls of Jerusalem. If there was ever a character in the Bible I needed to get to know as I worked to bring restoration to my barrio, it was Nehemiah.

NEHEMIAH'S BURDEN FOR JERUSALEM

In late autumn, in the month of Kislev, in the twentieth year of King Artaxerxes' reign, I was at the fortress of Susa. Hanani, one of my brothers, came to visit me with some other men who had just arrived from Judah. I asked them about the Jews who had returned there from captivity and about how things were going in Jerusalem.

They said to me, "Things are not going well for those who returned to the province of Judah. They are in great trouble and disgrace. The wall of Jerusalem has been torn down, and the gates have been destroyed by fire."

When I heard this, I sat down and wept. In fact, for days I mourned, fasted, and prayed to the God of heaven. (Nehemiah 1:1-4)

I imagine that Nehemiah had learned to deal with his identity issues as a minority born in the Persian Empire in much the same way that I did growing up as a Mexican American in the United States. He knew he had to fully understand the dominant culture's way of thinking and doing business in order to excel. He was intelligent, hard working, trustworthy and destined to succeed. When we encounter Nehemiah in chapter 1, he is the cupbearer to King Artaxerxes—an executive-level position with extreme responsibilities. He was not only the king's protector who carefully selected and tasted the food and wine that the king and the royal family would consume, but he was also one of Artaxerxes's most trusted advisers on matters big and small. Nehemiah had risen in leadership and influence in the Persian Empire in spite of his status as a Jew. He excelled at his job, and he had the backing and support of the king's wife. He was a man of faith who loved and worshiped the God of his ancestors, and he faithfully and contently served in the king's palace, far removed from the troubles of Jerusalem.

I am certain that today many excellent nonwhite leaders struggle with the kind of predicament Nehemiah found himself in as a key leader in the Persian government. They have excelled in school, graduated at the top of their class and risen to the top of their professions or disciplines. If they are serious about their faith, they often have to discern how to stay connected to their roots while continuing to develop and advance in their careers. Like Nehemiah, many of these young Christian leaders find themselves in high places wondering why God has placed them there. Getting too comfortable and too removed from their community is an ever-present danger.

For Nehemiah, that all began to change when his brother Hanani returned from Judah and gave him an eyewitness report about the troubles that befell their fellow Jews in Jerusalem. Even with the influx of men, women and children returning to the city of peace from exile, the city was in shambles. The walls of the city were torn down and the gates destroyed by fire, leaving everyone vulnerable and in disgrace. Nehemiah wondered how the holy city could still be experiencing this kind of devastation.

When he heard this horrible report from his brother, Nehemiah doubled over and began to weep uncontrollably. This was not the first time he had caught wind of the problems that existed in Jerusalem, but for some reason this time he could not disregard what he had just heard. He prayed and fasted for days. He felt the pain and agony of his people, and overcome by grief and sorrow he cried out to God. God was stirring something in his heart; Nehemiah felt a deep burden in his soul to go to Jerusalem and rebuild the broken walls.

I resonated greatly with Nehemiah and with his God-given assignment. I identified with his unshakable call to return to Jerusalem once he learned about the suffering of the people who lived there. He knew that Ezra, the priest and teacher of the Law, was there and might feel threatened by his arrival, but he was determined to exercise his leadership to get the walls repaired and restored. While he cared greatly about the spiritual condition of the people in Jerusalem, his God-given assignment was to deal with the broken infrastructure of the city—the walls that were torn down. He arrived in Jerusalem with a bold vision to see it become a vibrant and flourishing city once more. Instead of devising a plan to ship in food and provide temporary relief for his Jewish brothers and sisters, he planned the restoration and development of the entire city (see fig. 5).

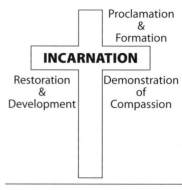

I resonated so deeply with Nehemiah's burden when I arrived in La Villita, and I still do twenty-five years later as I work with amazing leaders committed to living and

Figure 5

ministering in cities devastated by poverty. Like Nehemiah, I have cried, prayed and created grand plans to engage Christians in the work of community revitalization around the country. I have seen others gripped with this same burden spend years alongside their neighbors, investing their lives to create healthier neighborhoods. Their motivation comes directly from God.

Nehemiah finally approached the king after four long months of prayer, planning and preparation. He knew what needed to be done; he needed to take a leave of absence from his government job to take on this assignment; he needed letters of passage from the king to guarantee safe travels; he needed building materials and skilled laborers to lead the construction project; he needed political power—being appointed governor of the region would be ideal; and he needed the mighty intervention of God. Everything he asked for was granted, and before he knew it, he was on his way to Jerusalem as an agent of the king and the one true King. Upon arriving in Jerusalem, Nehemiah constructed his own residence in the city and implemented his plan to rebuild the broken walls.

I too was as committed as ever to figuring out how to make our barrio a healthier place to live, not for outsiders like in Cabrini Green but for our very own residents. I was ecstatic that more families were joining our growing church and that the after-school program we started was putting us in contact with even more parents to reach for Christ. Yet everyone who knew me was aware that I was just as excited about working on the restoration and development of the physical environment of our neighborhood as I was about pastoring our church. In the same way that Nehemiah had been called to work in Jerusalem many years before, I felt a deep burden to see our barrio become a healthy place for families to call home.

A NEW LEADERSHIP APPROACH

Sanballat was very angry when he learned that we were rebuilding the wall. He flew into a rage and mocked the Jews, saying in front of his friends and the Samaritan army officers, "What does this bunch of poor, feeble Jews think they're doing? Do they think they can build the wall in a single day by just offering a few sacrifices? Do they actually think they can make something of stones from a rubbish heap—and charred ones at that?"

Tobiah the Ammonite, who was standing beside him, remarked, "That stone wall would collapse if even a fox walked along the top of it!" (Nehemiah 4:1-3)

So the wall was completed on the twenty-fifth of Elul, in fifty-two days. (Nehemiah 6:15 NIV)

When the word began to spread in Jerusalem that the king's envoy was on its way to the city, it must have created the kind of buzz that Chicago experiences when President Obama comes home for a visit. When Ezra came years before, the Samaritans were not too nervous about another rabbi coming into town. However, when Nehemiah came with the might of the Persian army behind him, it was a different story. Nobody was certain why Nehemiah and his entourage had been sent, but everybody paid attention (Nehemiah 2:16). It could be that the king wanted tighter control of the region against revolt or that he wanted to collect more taxes. But no one could have imagined what Nehemiah was about to do. With his plans in hand, and his heart still pounding from getting the king's approval for his brazen proposal, Nehemiah was determined to make the most of this opportunity to do good for his people and for his God.

Nehemiah was aware that not only were the walls of the city broken but the political system was broken as well. Sanballat, Tobiah and other enemies of Jerusalem constantly threatened the well-being of the Jews, and they were intent on the city's destruction for their own gain. When they caught wind of Nehemiah's audacious plan, they were disturbed that this powerful do-gooder would sabotage the stronghold they had on the city. With no time to waste, Nehemiah surveyed the broken walls and devised a master plan. He declared that the old way of doing business was over. Under his new administration, there would be no more bribes or outlandish perks for anyone on his government payroll. From now on the priority was the completion of the project, and not the personal gain of a few fat cats. This was a good way to make enemies and to get the people fired up—they had not seen a leader like Nehemiah come around for a very long time.

Not only was Nehemiah committed to leading and working with integrity, but he was also determined to engage every family who could work in the rebuilding of the wall (Nehemiah 3). If success was to be had, it was essential to have grassroots involvement at every level. Finally, bold and effective leadership was being exercised for the sake of the city, and the walls of Jerusalem were rebuilt in just fifty-two days.

Unlike in North Lawndale, where Coach and his amazing crew were effectively working to rebuild a neighborhood that had shrunk in population from over 120,000 residents to under 50,000 in four decades, and where businesses were almost non-existent except for a few liquor stores and check-cashing outlets, we had so much to build on in La Villita. I was determined to begin our community-development work, but I was venturing into uncharted waters. I was more experienced sharing my faith and demonstrating compassion toward those in need than I was executing a development project. My education and training were in art and theology, and I knew virtually nothing about real estate or business development (although I did handle the role of general contractor when I rehabbed my homes). I relied heavily on the example of Coach and the Lawndale ministries to be my guide, and what I lacked in formal training I was ready to make up for with my enthusiasm and passion.

I took time to listen to the residents of the community, to our church members and to key leaders about their hopes and dreams for La Villita. Everyday, I got more excited about launching into the work of creating a flourishing community alongside of our neighbors. Surprisingly, unlike Nehemiah, we received little opposition or resistance from the local alderman or from any of the key community leaders. Instead, much of the opposition I received came from within the ranks of our church leadership. Trying to lead both the church and our community-development efforts was catching up to me, and it was creating significant tension in our ministry.

Pressing forward, we established a nonprofit organization, *Nueva Creación*, to function as the community-development arm of our church. Before our incorporation process was completed, I received a call from a staff person from World Vision requesting a meeting. They had started a new program to develop affordable housing in Chicago, and they wanted to find a partner in the Latino community. They found out about our budding ministry and were interested in supporting our work. In a very short time we were drawing up the papers to receive a $50,000 grant to start a low-income housing program, and I was thrown into the world of urban development, putting me in regular contact with lawyers, construction contractors, bankers and city inspectors.

By 1996 my life was inundated with endless opportunities, mounting responsibilities and ever-increasing stress and tension. We had a growing church, a massive, old building that needed to be rehabbed and a new housing ministry that needed my attention. I had a wife and three small children who needed me, and I was becoming more involved in the leadership of CCDA. The year before, I was elected to the board of directors of CCDA after delivering a talk in Detroit titled "Mo Color Mo Better," in which I reminded the audience that we were called to radical expressions of racial reconciliation. A year later at our Denver CCDA conference, I gave a keynote address titled "Making Great Salsa in the Barrios of our Nation." In my talk I laid out a biblical recipe for restoring under-resourced communities, which emphasized the need to keep Jesus as our main ingredient in everything we did.

My good friend and fellow board member Glen Kehrien, who has since gone on to be with the Lord, recommended that I become a speaker for the Promise Keepers men's movement, and over the next few years I spoke in over twenty-five stadiums filled with thousands of men on the topic of racial reconciliation. On Saturday I would speak to thousands of rowdy guys in stadiums, and then I would return to Chicago on Sunday to preach in my tiny barrio church with less than two hundred people in attendance.

I was in desperate need of focus, wisdom and direction as I juggled the demands of being a local pastor, a community developer and now a national speaker. I was aware that my passion was to be a Nehemiah leader in La Villita, yet I clung to my role as the Ezra of our ministry as well.

A NEW PARTNERSHIP WITH EZRA

> Then Nehemiah the governor, Ezra the priest and teacher of the Law, and the Levites who were instructing the people said to them all, "This day is holy to the LORD your God. Do not mourn or weep." For all the people had been weeping as they listened to the words of the Law. (Nehemiah 8:9 NIV)

Thanks to the leadership of Nehemiah, Jerusalem had a physical wall to protect the residents of the city. Next it was time for Ezra to restore the people's spiritual vibrancy and commitment, knowing that they had to be strengthened internally if they were ever going to flourish. Years before, God had called Ezra to return to Jerusalem to revive the temple. Finally, he was fulfilling the dream that he had once held for the spiritual revival of his people. One of the first issues Ezra took on was that all the Jewish men should divorce their non-Jewish wives or have them convert to Judaism. Whoever refused would be excluded from the community. For the sake of spiritual survival, no compromises could be made. Then he addressed the Sabbath desecration. The Jewish shop owners had in many cases found legal loopholes to conduct their work on the day of rest. Ezra passed decrees closing the loopholes and thus eliminating Sabbath work.

Ultimately, Ezra and Nehemiah called the people together and reinstated what became known as "The Covenant of Faith" (Nehemiah 9:38). The people read from the book of Deuteronomy, which described all of the laws and ideals they were not living up to. They all wept, repented and agreed to uphold the Torah from that time on—especially to observe the Sabbath, to bring the tithes and donations to the temple and to refrain from intermarriage.

Working together, Ezra and Nehemiah made unbelievable progress in restoring Jerusalem. Until Nehemiah arrived on the scene, Ezra had been stymied in his ability to revive the people's faith. Their partnership made all the difference in the world! Still, with all of its recent improvements, the city of Jerusalem needed their ongoing leadership and attention for years to come.

When Robert Guerrero joined our team to be my ministry partner, I was certain I had found the Ezra I was looking for! I had never been around a leader with so much passion for the proclamation of the good news and the formation of new believers. We would spend many hours together praying, strategizing and hanging out as brothers. Even though he was Dominican and I was Mexican, we made a great team. While I was mentoring him on the basic principles of Christian community development, he was already deeply committed to the holistic approach to ministry that we were developing in La Villita. I imagined that Robert and I would be working together for years to come.

As often happens in ministry when a group of people are pursuing a vision from God, our work in La Villita began to experience spiritual attacks. The biggest blow came when Robert and his wife began to experience some serious marital problems. After a few excruciating months of counseling sessions and prayer, they decided to return to the Dominican Republic to work on their marriage. I fully supported their decision, but I had lost my Ezra and was overwhelmed with grief and disappointment. We had an amazing collection of leaders that had relocated to the neighborhood and a growing number of Mexican leaders from the community providing leadership for our ministry, but I was reeling from the loss of my partner. As a result of my discouragement, I often failed to provide the kind of effective, Ezra-like leadership that was desperately needed to keep such a diverse, multicultural group of individuals working together as a church.

With the growing realization that I was wired like Nehemiah, I began to look for ways to identify another pastor and partner, an Ezra, to help me carry the load.

A NEW OCCUPY MOVEMENT

Now the city was large and spacious, but there were few people in it, and the houses had not yet been rebuilt. (Nehemiah 7:4 NIV)

Now the leaders of the people settled in Jerusalem. The rest of the people cast lots to bring one out of every ten of them to live in Jerusalem, the holy city, while the remaining nine were to stay in their own towns. The people commended all who volunteered to live in Jerusalem. (Nehemiah 11:1-2 NIV)

Having spent his life living and working in Susa, Nehemiah had experienced firsthand what it was like to live in a healthy, secure community. Before relocating to Jerusalem, he had a stressful but very successful career. By all accounts he was living the Persian dream, which must have felt unattainable to most of his fellow Jews still living in exile in Babylon. He was well-educated, had a great job and probably had no intentions of moving to the barrio of Jerusalem.

Unexpectedly, he was now in Jerusalem living in the 'hood as the politically appointed representative of the king of Persia. After completing his initial goal of rebuilding the walls of the city in just fifty-two days, he realized that his job was not complete. The walls were no longer vulnerable, but it would take another decade of working with the residents of the city to reform their way of thinking and empower them politically. It would also take that long to support Ezra in his renewed efforts to revitalize the spiritual lives of the Jewish people who had been unfaithful to God for years.

With the walls solidified and Ezra leading the people in a time of spiritual revival, Nehemiah knew they needed to repopulate the city with godly Jewish families who could add to the stability and growth of Jerusalem. Nehemiah instructed the Jewish residents in the areas surrounding Jerusalem to draw lots to identify those chosen by God to relocate in Jerusalem. This bold and strategic move would accelerate the sustainability of Jerusalem. With additional families returning to the city, new businesses would be established, homes would be filled with the smell of food and with laughter, schools would overflow with children, and the temple would be the center of worship and community pride. Nehemiah's dream was becoming a reality.

At the end of twelve years in the city, Nehemiah returned home to Persia, where he must have spent hours debriefing the king and his fellow Jews. During his time away from Jerusalem, Nehemiah began to hear reports that trouble was brewing back in the city. The residents' commitment to God was floundering. Devastated, concerned for their well-being, and wanting to support Ezra and his brother, who was now serving as the governor of Judah, Nehemiah returned once again to take the leadership reins of the city he had grown to love. The work of restoring a vulnerable community was messy and required a long-term commitment.

After almost a decade of being in La Villita, we were beginning to see more and more families move into the community, but it was not an easy sell. Our Mexican members who had worked hard to escape the barrio of La Villita found it difficult to consider returning for the sake of the ministry. Our inspiration was Lawndale Community Church, who had sent many of their young people to college only for them to return upon graduation to connect with the church and its vision to revitalize their community. We wanted to see the same thing happen in La Villita, but it would take time.

Whenever members were able to purchase their own home, it was a victory. I was especially inspired when I found out that two single mothers from our church made the decision to buy homes in La Villita instead of moving away into nicer or safer communities. They had become fully invested in the vision of loving and restoring our barrio. I was encouraged that if Aurelia and Juanita could take this bold step of faith, others could as well, not because they had drawn a short lot but because the Spirit of God had put a burden in their hearts to do so.

With Nehemiah as my inspiration, I was certain it was only a matter of time before La Villita would become a flourishing community pleasing to God.

NINE

Confrontation of Injustice

It was difficult not to be inspired by how hard Leticia worked to provide
for her children. She was a very dignified woman with a warm
smile that defied how tough she was. She had become very serious about her new faith in Christ and was always on time for
our church service on Sunday mornings, even though she often
walked with her kids close to a mile in the rain or snow. Her
beautiful daughters with their frilly lace and handsome son with
his stylish tie were always the best-dressed children at church. As
I got to know Letty, I found out she was an entrepreneur. She
made and sold tamales every day in the neighborhood. Like my
grandmother, she worked herself to exhaustion to provide for her
kids. Every morning, long before the roosters in our barrio began
to crow, Letty would prepare the *pollo* (chicken), *puerco* (pork)
and *masa* (dough) she needed to make the tamales she would sell
later that morning. By 5 a.m. she would be on 31st Street in her
designated spot. Day in and day out, she provided her delicious
tamales to the men and women heading to work in factories, res-
taurants and hotels. Even the day laborers who gathered at the
Home Depot, praying to be picked up by someone looking for
cheap labor, stopped to buy their breakfast from Letty. After she

sold every last tamale, she rushed home in time to dress her children and send them off to school. She faithfully repeated this process day after day.

Ironically, Mexicans are known to be some of the hardest-working immigrants in our nation. The stereotype of the "lazy Mexican" taking a *siesta* (afternoon nap), as he leans against a cactus could not be further from the truth. Ask any contractor or factory owner, and they will tell you they are excited to have an entire crew of Mexican workers. Hard work is the only honorable option men and women without legal immigration status have in this country.

The most valuable commodity in our immigrant community is our hard-working men and women. Yet, with all of the *ganas* (effort) that my neighbors invest, they seem to barely get by economically. Often, parents are forced to leave their teenagers unattended for hours as they work double shifts to make ends meet. In many instances, this leads to mischief and gang involvement.

As we developed our strategy as a church to seek shalom and the well-being of our community, we invested most of our resources on supporting our children. Whenever we spoke to the parents about their aspirations, they would inevitably talk to us about their children. Like all parents, they wanted a better life for their kids and were willing to sacrifice their own needs and wants to make this happen. I was convinced that with our community's work ethic we could find ways to identify or create better paying jobs, get our young people into college, provide our families with opportunities for homeownership, and help our neighbors find authentic faith in Jesus Christ.

We were on the right track to creating a healthier community. A growing number of church members living in our barrio were committed to loving their neighbors. Our church was committed to being a witness for Christ in the community. We had programs to combat gang violence and to reach our youth. Small business loans were being offered to our members. We were starting a homeownership program in our community. Educational and summer programs were developed to support our kids and draw them close to Christ. Families were being healed and transformed. We were doing everything we could to live out the principles of Christian community development in our Mexican barrio.

My friend Fernando was always working, and he always seemed to be looking for a better job. I later found out that he had studied civil engineering in Mexico. Here in the United States he worked wherever he could find a job to feed his family, mostly in low-paying construction jobs. He was very eager to grow in his faith, so it was not unusual for him to come by my house or the church office to talk. As I learned about his life, I got an education about our nation's immigration system. I knew that the majority of the residents in La Villita were first-generation Mexican immigrants, but I had no idea that so many of my neighbors had entered our country illegally.

Like Fernando, who came to *El Norte* (North) seeking a better life for his family, many of his friends and neighbors in La Villita did the same thing. They heard about our large Mexican community in Chicago from a friend or relative and were assured that if they were able to get across the border, they would be able to find a job much better than what they could find in Mexico. If they were fortunate, they would find a way to get their papers, but immediate survival was their primary concern.

Fernando's story was not an exception but the norm in my barrio. I could not believe I was not more aware of this situation. In 1986, when President Reagan passed his now infamous immigration amnesty bill that legally integrated close to three million undocumented immigrants into our nation, my ministry was narrowly focused on evangelizing and discipling young people in San Jose. Nevertheless, while that bill helped millions of people get papers so they could work, it did not adequately address the needed changes in our immigration policy to assure that we would not be in the same situation in the future. The future is now, and today we have over 11 million undocumented immigrants in our nation, many of them worshiping in churches throughout our nation.

Trying to wrap my mind around the immigration struggles of my friends and neighbors overwhelmed me. I often asked the Lord why I was so blessed to have been born just a few miles north of the border as a US citizen. Determined to find a way to help my friends with this issue, I connected a number of our undocumented neighbors with the office of World Relief, where one of our church members, Galen Carey, was the director. We were ready to pay whatever fees were needed to help our friends get the legal documentation they needed to put this issue behind them. What we found instead was a broken immigration system that made it almost impossible for individuals coming into our country because of economic hardship to get their legal status.

When I moved into our barrio years before, I never intended to get involved in a huge justice issue like immigration reform, nor was I looking for a cause beyond my neighborhood in which to invest my time. My initial motivation was to reach my neighbors with the good news of Jesus Christ and to mobilize my community to create a healthy, flourishing place to live. As time went on I heard many stories from church members about the hardships of living and working in the shadows of our society. Without legal status, they were often taken advantage of by their employers and endured other

Figure 6

types of abuse as well. Families were devastated by deportations. All of these reports were impossible to ignore. I finally accepted the reality that in order to truly help my immigrant brothers and sisters caught in the web of our broken system, I needed to add an essential component to my ministry—the confrontation of injustice (see fig. 6). Instead of simply blaming my undocumented friends for crossing the border to seek a better life without legal standing, I had to come to grips with the reality that our nation's immigration policy enabled and encouraged this illegal migration, which ultimately benefited our economy. Our immigration system is broken, and millions of men, women and children are being negatively affected. A change is desperately needed.

Because I was incarnated in the community, living side by side with my undocumented brothers and sisters, I realized that inviting them to one more Bible study, providing them with another bag of groceries or even establishing another program to bolster their education would not adequately address their immigration status in our country. The fact that my undocumented friends were in our nation illegally was a lose-lose situation for everybody, and I was determined to do whatever was necessary to bring about change to our current immigration system. Unexpectedly, I found myself working to reform our national immigration policy as an extension of my local ministry.

The more I got involved and informed about our broken immigration system, the more it caused me to reexamine my theology and understanding related to justice in the Bible. Not only did I find many references in the Bible to underscore God's concern for the stranger and the alien, but I began to connect the need to confront injustice with the Scripture's emphasis on God's love for the poor and the vulnerable. I was already convinced that as Christians we are called to love and serve the poor in their distress, but now I realized that the most vulnerable people are often victims of oppression and injustice. Not just individuals need to be confronted with their sin, but broken and fallen systems need to be confronted and changed as well.

The prophet Amos articulates the kind of suffering and abuse that undocumented people regularly have to endure. Amos helped me to consider how to advocate for them more effectively. I was struck by God's desire for all those created in his image to experience his love and his justice. Oppression of any kind is an abomination in the eyes of God, and as his follower I am responsible for confronting the injustice of our broken immigration system. The words of the prophet Amos were impossible to ignore:

> You trample the poor,
>   stealing their grain through taxes and unfair rent.
> Therefore, though you build beautiful stone houses,
>   you will never live in them.
> Though you plant lush vineyards,
>   you will never drink wine from them.
> For I know the vast number of your sins
>   and the depth of your rebellions.
> You oppress good people by taking bribes
>   and deprive the poor of justice in the courts. (Amos
>   5:11-12)

As I became more serious about addressing the systemic problems in our immigration policy, I was convinced that it was not just the unlawful behavior of undocumented individuals that was at fault, but in fact our entire economic system was complicit in creating the mess we are in. Large segments of our economic system are dependent on the cheap labor provided by undocumented workers, and now they are being scapegoated and blamed for every problem our nation experiences. Simultaneously, the terrorist attacks of 9/11 and the devastating crash of our economy in recent years has created a strong backlash against the growing numbers of undocumented immigrants in our nation.

The words of our CCDA lifetime board member Mary Nelson often come to mind: instead of focusing our efforts on pulling drowning people out of the river, we need to go upstream to find out who is pushing them into the water in the first place! Our work is not simply to put Band-Aids on issues that affect the poor but to dig deeper to address the root causes of poverty and injustice as essential components of kingdom ministry.

Along with being committed to helping my neighbors in La Villita come to faith in Christ, offering appropriate expressions of compassion and working to see my barrio flourish through community development efforts, I was now looking for ways to change our immigration laws at a national level. After reading Jim Wallis's book *God's Politics*, I took a trip to Washington, DC, to meet with him. He graciously agreed to meet, and I was able to ask why he did not address immigration in his book. He took that conversation to heart, and before too long Sojourners, a Christian ministry committed to faith in action for social justice of which Jim is president, became an important champion on this issue. I also reached out to a few prominent pastors to engage them in a conversation on the topic of immigration, but I received absolutely no response. I was finding out that the church has a long way to go in its understanding or concern for the undocumented immigrants in our nation.

In an effort to crystallize my own thinking about this new dimension of my ministry, I began to study the life and passion narrative of Christ. I found a compelling portrait of a God who absolutely loves and sides with the poor and the stranger in society—my undocumented neighbors.

THE PASSION OF CHRIST AND OUR UNDOCUMENTED NEIGHBORS

> You shall treat the stranger who sojourns with you as the native among you, and you shall love him as yourself, for you were strangers in the land of Egypt: I am the LORD your God. (Leviticus 19:34 ESV)

Leviticus 19:34 is a favorite among Christians who support immigration reform. This verse clearly calls God's people to treat strangers, or those who are not from their land, as one of their own. In fact, the Evangelical Immigration Table, which was formed in 2012 to help advocate for a biblical approach to immigration, put together a bookmark with forty Scripture verses that speak about God's concern for the immigrant. Our goal was to help Christians see for themselves that the Bible is not silent about this important issue. I contend that the Bible reveals a God who puts at the center of his love and concern those at the margins of society.

There is often a strong reaction by those of us who are wealthy and powerful (which includes the majority of us who live in America) to the idea that God could have a special concern for the poor and the vulnerable. Remembering God as a loving and concerned Father can help us to gain insight into this perspective. I am a parent of three children, and when one of my kids is in crisis or suffering, it is not difficult for me to leave the other two children on their own for a time while I give special attention to my sick or suffering child. This special love and concern does not exclude my other children from my love, but it does give priority to my ailing child. It seems Jesus consistently gives high priority to those who are alienated and without much hope.

Christ's redemptive work on the cross may be the most radical identification of God with the marginalized and humiliated. Hebrews 13:12 reminds us that Jesus was crucified outside the gates of Jerusalem in a place called Golgotha, which is where criminals and thieves were executed. So Jesus laid down his sinless life for the redemption of the entire world in this despised place on the margins of both religious and political power and respectability. The significance is startling: Jesus not only laid down his life but also his reputation. God allowed his only begotten Son to be murdered and crucified alongside criminals so everyone would understand that no one is beyond redemption or beyond inclusion in his kingdom.

I am shocked and appalled at the insults levied against undocumented men, women and children in our nation. Yes, they have broken laws to be in this country, but they also have been hired, used and often abused by employers and our economic system in need of cheap labor. Because of their vulnerable status, it has become common to scapegoat and hurl insults at them without regard to the fact that they are human beings created in the image of God. Most shocking is that these types of insults are sometimes made by those claiming to be followers of Christ.

In the last hours of Jesus' life, he was insulted and mocked by the crowds. The Bible says, "they hurled all sorts of terrible insults at him" (Luke 22:65). This verbal abuse is one way that Jesus is connected to our undocumented neighbors.

In Jesus' false conviction, beating, suffering and brutal death, everyone can see that his forgiving grace is for all, and that redemption is offered to all, regardless of the severity of our past trespasses or sinfulness. So, when we speak about God's love for the stranger, we are not basing it on one verse from an ancient text. Instead, it is a truth rooted in the entire revelation of God's salvific activity, which culminates on the cross. This indeed is good news to the poor, to the immigrants among us, and to all believers redeemed by the radical love of Jesus.

After years of working on this issue without much support from more conservative evangelical pastors, leaders or believers, in 2013 I began to see a dramatic shift. Support for immigration reform from the Roman Catholic and mainline church leaders has been strong for a long time. Finally, a dramatic change took place in the minds and hearts of respected evangelical leaders who discovered that God's love for the immigrant is a central theme in Scripture—a theme that had often been ignored. Christians as a whole are beginning to realize that loving and welcoming the strangers in our land is not a political statement but is being faithful to the gospel.

THE CURRENT STATUS OF IMMIGRATION REFORM

In spite of the growing concern and involvement by Christians who have begun to push our political leaders to fix our broken immigration system, we still do not have a new immigration policy in our nation. But it is impossible to deny that Christ-followers from diverse traditions have united to make immigration reform a moral, human rights and justice issue, which has surprised many people in our nation and in the Christian community. In fact, the Evangelical Immigration Table represents one of the most diverse and broad coalitions of evangelical Christians who have come together to work on a common cause.

What has united us is a common conviction that the men, women and children labeled as "illegals" by many in our nation are first and foremost human beings created in the image of God. God's love and concern for these individuals has awakened compassion and concern that has led to action in the streets of the barrios and in the halls of Congress.

A dozen principle organizations, including CCDA, are committed to working together until we see our nation reform our current system, which ultimately hurts people and our nation. Because of our nation's inability to pass legislation to address our broken immigration system, we face an unprecedented humanitarian crisis at the border. Thousands of children from Central America have been caught and detained as they attempt to enter our nation without their parents. Our government will have to process as many as ninety thousand children in 2014—the highest number of such cases in the history of our nation.

THE RESPONSE OF THE CHURCH

I recently returned from my birth town of Weslaco, Texas, which is just a few miles from where many of these children are being detained, processed and housed until they can be reunited with their families. By all accounts, it is a crisis of enormous proportion. It has compelled the president to seek billions of dollars in new funding to address this issue. It also has moved thousands of churches and Christ-followers to get involved. We are currently coordinating efforts to minister to these children, who have been traumatized making their way to our nation. They are often abused by *coyotes* (smugglers) or drug cartel leaders who bring these vulnerable children through Mexico to our border; the children face sexual assault, fatigue and hunger. Their suffering is unimaginable. Again we are reminded of Jesus' words in Matthew 25 that when we minister to hungry, naked and thirsty children, we minister to Christ himself.

Ultimately, my hope and prayer is that we will see a new national policy passed into law that will be more just and fair toward our immigrant brothers and sisters from every nation of the world. I pray that our standing for justice on behalf of these men, women and children will be a powerful witness to the love and compassion of Christ for those on the margins of society. At the end of time, I long to hear the words of Jesus: "I tell you the truth, when you did it to one of the least of these my brothers and sisters, you were doing it to me!" (Matthew 25:40)

After thirty years of following Christ and ministering in the barrios of our nation, I am convinced that how we treat our immigrant brothers and sisters is critical to the witness of the church. As we are gripped with the love and compassion of Christ, working for justice is an indispensable component of kingdom ministry.

One day I hope to share with my grandchildren the story of how a great number of Christ-followers, including myself, worked to bring about a new and more just immigration system in our society. I can't wait for that day to come!

MASS INCARCERATION

For the past three years my wife and I have made Lawndale Christian Community Church our home church.[1] We have key relationships there that go back twenty-five years, and I get to see the work of Christian community development lived out every day, as it is one of our model ministries. Not only is our CCDA national office located on the LCCC campus, but my wife, Marianne, works at the Lawndale Christian Health Center, which was started by the church almost thirty years ago. It does a better job of creating employment opportunities and fostering an environment for racial reconciliation than any ministry I know of in Chicago. It also provides our neighbors with excellent health care services, which includes a world-class fitness center.

On any given Sunday at our weekly worship service, we hear an announcement about the Hope House ministry and witness its impact. Typically fifty men recovering from drug addiction or who have returned from prison worship alongside hundreds of other members of the church each week. It's a sight to behold.

On Friendship Sunday, when folks are encouraged to share praise and prayer requests, someone inevitably requests prayer for a friend or family member who has been shot or locked up. The issue of mass incarceration impacts the lives of our neighbors in North Lawndale and La Villita at an alarming rate. The Cook

County Jail, which is located just a half mile from my house, is a revolving door for black and Latino men waiting for trial or to do time in federal prison, many for drug-related issues.

The statistics are startling. The United States is the world's leader in incarceration with 2.2 million people currently in the nation's prisons or jails, a 500 percent increase over the past thirty years. These trends have resulted in prison overcrowding and with state governments being overwhelmed by the burden of funding a rapidly expanding penal system, despite increasing evidence that large-scale incarceration is not the most effective means of achieving public safety.

Unbelievably, more African Americans are under the control of the criminal justice system today than were enslaved in 1850. And once someone becomes a felon, it becomes almost impossible to regain solid footing in society in terms of employment or civic involvement. The stigma of being a felon is almost impossible to overcome.

Since many more people of color than whites are felons, racial discrimination remains as powerful as it was under slavery or under the postslavery era of Jim Crow segregation. The Sentencing Project's April 2014 sentencing brief observes,

> The dramatic growth of the U.S. prison population in the last 40 years has led to record levels of disenfranchisement, with an estimated 5.85 million voters banned from the polls today. Disenfranchisement policies vary widely by state, ranging from no restrictions on voting to a lifetime ban upon conviction. Felony disenfranchisement has potentially affected the outcomes of U.S. elections, particularly as disenfranchisement policies disproportionately affect people of color. Nationwide, one in every 13 black adults cannot vote because of a felony conviction, and in three

states—Florida, Kentucky and Virginia—more than one in five black adults is disenfranchised.[2]

Last year Michelle Alexander, author of *The New Jim Crow: Mass Incarceration in the Age of Colorblindness,* spoke at our national CCDA conference in New Orleans. Alexander described how mass incarceration today serves the same purpose as pre–Civil War slavery and the post–Civil War Jim Crow laws, which is to maintain a racial caste system. The original Jim Crow laws, after slavery ended, promoted racial discrimination in public housing, employment, voting and education. Alexander asserts that the racial caste system has not ended but has been redesigned. The new Jim Crow is tied to a penal system that is systematically devastating minority communities in cities like Chicago.

In her talk, Alexander explained how the criminal justice system functions as a new system of racial control by targeting black men through the "War on Drugs." The Anti-Drug Abuse Act of 1986, for example, includes far more severe punishment for distribution of crack cocaine (associated with blacks) than powder cocaine (associated with whites). Civil penalties, such as not being able to live in public housing and not being able to get student loans, have been added to the already harsh prison sentences.

"Today," says Alexander, "a criminal freed from prison has scarcely more rights, and arguably less respect, than a freed slave or a black person living 'free' in Mississippi at the height of Jim Crow."[3]

Michelle Alexander is a powerful voice, joined by thousands of clergy and lay leaders around the nation, calling for the end of mass incarceration as we know it today. Many CCDA leaders have gotten involved, realizing that unless we work to reform our broken incarceration system, which disproportionately disenfranchises brown and black men, our communities will never prosper or flourish.

I know that it is difficult for most white, middle-class Americans to grasp how unjust our current incarceration system is. The majority of suburban Christians have never been pulled over by a hostile police officer primarily because of the color of their skin or because of the neighborhood they live in. These are experiences that men in our communities face on a regular basis.

My middle son, Stefan, is a clean-cut, dark-skinned young man who graduated from college and now works at a downtown Chicago social media company not far from the North Shore, a very ritzy section of North Chicago. Recently, after leaving work, he was walking outside of his office to meet some friends when a police officer stopped to question him for no other reason than being brown. This clearly upset Stefan, and it is the kind of harassment young Latino and African American men endure in our society.

Instead of simply continuing to minister to inmates in prison or providing aftercare once men are out of the penitentiary, we are now convinced that working to confront and reform the unjust mass incarceration system in our country is a component of kingdom ministry we must engage in. As we have acted on the issue of immigration, we are determined to foster policy changes nationally related to mass incarceration that will bring justice to our neighbors.

EDUCATION REFORM

Perhaps the most significant justice issue many of our poor communities face is an inequitable education system that fails the majority of poor children, especially children of color.

In many inner-city school districts across the country, children are not reading at their grade level, the achievement gap is widening, and too many African American and Latino students are not graduating from high school. Teachers in most urban school districts like Chicago feel powerless to stem this tide of educational decline, and they often feel the blame of administrators, politicians, parents and the media for the underperformance of so many students.

At one of our recent CCDA conferences, Nichole Baker Fulgham, who used to lead the faith-based work of Teach for America and is now the founder and president of the Expectations Project—an organization focused on mobilizing faith communities to close the academic achievement gap in US public education—has helped us to see the huge challenges that our children face when they do not get a solid education.

Our CCDA ministries across the country have been involved in this work for decades. Our ministries have started schools, opened up after-school programs, offered support for teachers, adopted entire schools and offered scholarships to low-income students to attend college. One ministry from the Bay Area has provided scholarships to hundreds of graduates, helping them gain entry into top colleges, supporting them until they graduate. At Lawndale Christian Community Church, over two hundred students have attended college and then returned to live and work in the community.

Now, we are asking deeper questions about how to fundamentally change the ways that we deliver public education in poor communities and how to develop more supportive and flourishing communities so that every child can get a quality education in a safe environment.

Education reform is seen as a civil rights issue in our day, and we have to be involved.

Without being incarnated in the community, we would not know what issues to advocate or how to advocate in a way that empowers those affected by these issues to lead the charge. Ultimately, our prayer is that God's justice would flow like a mighty stream in the most vulnerable neighborhoods of our nation.

Wherever we see these injustices, we have to get involved.
We will pray.
We will work to understand the issues.
We will organize our neighbors to get involved.
We will protest if necessary to bring light to injustice.
We will advocate for better policies.

TEN

Sí, Se Puede

Around the time my family was leaving behind our life along the US-Mexican border to strike middle-class gold near what is now the Silicon Valley, Cesar Chavez was beginning to unionize mostly Mexican American farm workers in the Central Valley of California, seeking to ensure fair wages and humane working conditions. His grape boycotts and nonviolent action, which included hunger strikes and marches, have been an inspiration to me as a Chicano with a heart for *justicia*. During one of his grape boycotts in the mid-1980s, right before I got married, I decided to boycott grapes myself and I have not eaten a grape since to remind me of my own calling to minister to the marginalized.

When Chavez died of natural causes in 1993 in his home state of Arizona, I remember being riveted to the TV as I watched his nationally televised funeral. Thousands of farm workers, dignitaries and what my good friend Juan Hernandez calls VIPs (Very Important *Paisanos* [compatriots]) lined the streets of Delano, California, where he was put to rest. I was most impressed with the fact that Cesar Chavez was buried in a coffin made of plain pine wood. Even in his burial, he would be identified with the poor and the humble. I long to see God raise up more leaders like Cesar Chavez and Oscar Romero to be agents of justice and love in our world.

At the time of Chavez's passing, I was in what I call the *Sí, se puede* years of our ministry in La Villita. Everything seemed possible. In my wildest dreams, I could never have imagined all of the struggles and conflicts that we would experience as a church.

More than ten years after arriving in La Villita with a burden for this barrio and for its people, we had a church with a compelling vision and committed members, but our church was struggling to survive. A few years earlier, we had merged with a small church in the community led by a Mexican American pastor who joined our team. Victor and his family lived in the community, but were new to the vision of Christian community development. Merging our church cultures was a challenge, and we struggled to come together as a new expression of the church we had started years ago. I finally had to admit that at the heart of our struggles was my leadership as pastor of the church. I was more convinced than ever that I needed to transition out of my Ezra role, but it was emotionally excruciating to do so with grace.

To make matters even more complicated, eventually we began to have serious conversations with a large church in the city that was beginning to initiate a multisite strategy in numerous communities of Chicago. I was desperate to find a way to step away from the pastorate, and we made the decision to become the La Villita site of New Life Community Church. The plan was that I would step into a Nehemiah role for all of their multiple congregations, helping them to engage in community development, but that plan never materialized. Instead, we experienced the kind of turmoil that was all too familiar in the early church, which the apostle Paul dealt with as he established churches throughout the Roman Empire—immature leadership, hurt feelings and stinging divisions that became unbearable. In spite of having great visions and dreams for the ministry we had started over a decade earlier, it was time for me to walk away from the church, wondering what had gone wrong.

When all of the dust settled, there were now two congregations in my barrio, La Villita Community Church and Nueva Vida–La Villita, committed to ministering in the community. Our family attended La Villita Community Church for a while after we transitioned out of my leadership role at the church, but we eventually settled at our current church home, Lawndale Christian Community Church, pastored by my good friend Coach Gordon. By the grace of God, twenty-five years after arriving in La Villita, the two congregations in La Villita continue to be vital witnesses for the kingdom in our barrio.

While it was an extremely discouraging time for me, the call and the burden that God had instilled in my heart for those on the margins of society was alive and well. The only thing in question was how I would live out this calling.

Over the next two years I had the privilege of consulting with the DeVos Urban Leadership Initiative, which was designed to invest in urban youth workers. The very thing this program was designed to do—help leaders become healthier and more effective—was what I needed most in my own life. I had to lead from my own brokenness as I was still recovering from my time at La Villita. I experienced amazing healing while serving as the program director for two years while the initiative was still being formalized.

At the end of my stint with DeVos, I signed on to help lead a new church plant with the Evangelical Covenant Church, not far from La Villita, with a vision to launch a multicultural church. My good friend Jonathan Hancock, others and I did our best to help a small group of leaders mobilized get this new effort started, until we realized that it would be best for everyone involved to not move forward with our fledgling endeavor. Once again, I found myself at a critical juncture in my life and ministry with no clear path in sight. The only certainty I had was that all of the stress I was experiencing was taking its toll on my health.

On a beautiful summer night around the time I was finishing my work with the Covenant denomination, I got some tickets to a ball game from one of my friends who played for the Chicago Cubs. My sons and I were sitting along the first base line a few rows back, and I found myself straining to read the scoreboard at Wrigley Field (it's a pretty good bet that the Cubs were losing). By the end of the game I was visiting the bathroom constantly. The next day I dropped in on my eye doctor friend at the Lawndale Clinic and told him I needed glasses. He asked me how long I had been having problems, and I told him that my vision began to blur the night before. Worried, he immediately sent me to be checked for diabetes. Sure enough, I was diagnosed with type 2 diabetes. That was all I needed, a major heath problem to go with all of my ministry issues!

God had grabbed my attention, and I was desperate for a positive turn in my life. About this time the Christian Community Development Association was beginning a national search for the director of their new CCDA Institute who would provide training for our members around the nation. Gordon Murphy, who supported the visionary leadership of Coach Gordon, John Perkins and the board, was doing a great job of stabilizing the national office and the funding base of CCDA. Coach was very aware of all that I had gone through in the previous years and encouraged me to apply for this new staff position at CCDA.

To my surprise, I was hired to lead the CCDA Institute, and I threw every ounce of my energy and passion into making this new venture a success. I loved CCDA and I was absolutely committed to our mission and vision as an association. We continued to live in La Villita, but the scope of my ministry was expanding into cities throughout the United States. I was finally ready to start a new chapter in my life, working to support and encourage leaders on the frontlines of this ministry.

RUNNING FOR MY LIFE

The work of getting the institute off the ground was every bit as exhilarating as I imagined. I traveled to dozens of cities to train our leaders and members in the "Eight Key Components" of Christian community development. This gave me the opportunity to get to know many of our stellar practitioners throughout the country, and day by day I discovered that I had finally found the one thing in life I was created to do—to train, equip and encourage men and women committed to ministering to the poor and marginalized of our world. I was feeling alive and revived.

At the same time that my role with CCDA was expanding, my waistline was expanding as well. I was not doing a good job of managing my diabetes. I knew I needed to get healthier, but I was at a total loss on how to do it. I was convinced that my eating habits were not terrible, although I loved *pan dulce* (sweet bread) and double Whoppers with cheese, and I was getting zero exercise. On a road trip from Phoenix to Los Angeles, I stopped at an all-you-can-eat buffet for lunch. At the end of my hefty meal, I made one final stop to gas up my car before hitting the road. Inside the station I picked up a book called *Overcoming Runaway Blood Sugar* by Dennis Pollock, which turned my life upside down. I'm not sure why, but this book motivated me to finally begin to change my eating habits and to start walking. After six months I was running on a regular basis. Within a year I had lost close to forty pounds, and my diabetes was under control. I felt so much better and had much more energy. I would need that new stamina; the leadership of CCDA asked me to take the role of Chief Executive Officer of our association just a few years after joining the staff.

TURNING FIFTY

Turning fifty was a milestone for me, and 2009 was a year to remember. That year I coedited a new book with my friend John Fuder titled *A Heart for the Community*. In this book we highlighted a variety of Chicagoland ministries connected to CCDA and Moody Bible Institute.

My oldest son Noel Luis and I completed the Los Angeles Marathon in May of that year as well. I made it across the finish line before the five-hour mark. It was hard to believe I had accomplished this after being so inactive for twenty years of my life. Running 26.2 miles gave me plenty of time to think and pray, and I thanked the Lord for how gracious he had been to carry me through the many valleys I had experienced throughout my life. I was so grateful for my amazing wife Marianne and for my marriage. I was so grateful for my kids Noel Luis, Stefan and Anna. I was so grateful for my parents, my siblings Sylvia, Veronica and Rey, and for my entire extended family—especially my mother-in-law, Rosemary, who loved me like her son. I was so grateful for all of my good friends and my teachers MaryJo and Bob, who loved and mentored me as a kid. I was so grateful for the opportunity I had to lead one of the most significant ministries in our nation. As I approached a huge incline at mile 17, I was extremely grateful to be coming to the end of the race. All I wanted was to make it up that hill and cross the finish line in one piece. Though I was tempted to quit at many stages along the way, I kept on pressing forward and finished the race!

That year my parents miraculously celebrated their fiftieth wedding anniversary. I had the privilege of being there with all of our family and with hundreds of friends as their pastor led them in renewing their vows. Growing up, I never expected I would live to see this day. During a private moment I had with their pastor, he made a comment that I could not believe: "If I had a hundred men like your father, we could change this city." I could not believe he was talking about my dad!

The next day Marianne, my parents and I went to the local mall to walk with other senior citizens of Modesto. After a couple of trips around the mall, Marianne and I stopped to grab some coffee, but my parents continued their walk. Out of the corner of my eye, I could have sworn I saw my parents walking hand in hand. I had never seen them show that kind of affection in public. I was finally ready to concede that God had invaded my father's heart and was reminded that no one was beyond the reach of his love and grace.

On Super Bowl Sunday of that long weekend, we were still in San Jose. During the Steelers–Cardinals game I received a phone call from Washington, DC. I didn't recognize the number and wondered who would be calling me on Sunday afternoon. I answered the phone and a woman named Mara Vanderslice said she was calling from the White House Office for Faith and Neighborhood Partnerships, which President Obama had just established. She asked if I would be willing to serve on this council for the upcoming year. I was stunned, but managed to say yes. What a way to cap off the year.

A VOICE FOR THE POOR AND THE FLAWED

On March 13, 2013, I was shocked when I first heard the announcement that the Catholic Church had elected a new pope, and that he was from Argentina. Very few of us knew very much about Jorge Mario Bergoglio, except that he was the first non-European pope in over one thousand years. And he was a Spanish-speaking Latino! To add to the intrigue, he took the name Francis, after Francis of Assisi, the patron saint of the poor, for his papal name. Unbelievable!

Since stepping into his role, Pope Francis has shaken up the

Roman Catholic establishment by forgoing the usual papal perks, which include red Gucci slippers and fancy limo processions. He has turned out to be the most important champion for the poor and the marginalized on the world stage since Mother Theresa, and people from every corner of the globe seem to be taking notice. It seems his humility and genuine connection with the homeless, the poor and the ostracized have marked him as a new kind of religious leader. Even those who have been most at odds with the teachings and doctrines of the church have become objects of his love and grace.

The insights that I have most appreciated from Pope Francis come from his personal creed about leadership, which is recorded in Chris Lowery's book *Pope Francis: Why He Leads the Way He Leads.* Lowery records three core convictions that form the foundation of the pope's leadership philosophy:

"I am flawed."
"I am a good and a gifted person."
"I am called to offer my gifts."[1]

Lowery concludes with this reflection on the Pope's thoughts:

Flawed, gifted and fundamentally good, and called: the three convictions are dynamically related. It is not merely, "Hey, I'm flawed. I'm arrogant and impossible to work with. But I've accepted myself, and I'm going to live authentically as my arrogant self. So you ought to accept me too." No, the call to leadership embeds not only acceptance of self but acceptance of the accountability to become the best possible version of oneself by addressing one's flaws relentlessly; the call to lead inspires that ongoing commitment to self improvement.[2]

As I have written this book, the acknowledgment that I am

flawed and a sinner in need of grace has been incredibly sobering but also liberating. Ironically, after spending so many years angry at my dad for his imperfections as a leader of our family, it turns out that my greatest regret in ministry has been my own inability to be a more effective pastor. It is humbling to accept that I have hurt and disappointed others in the same way that my own father has hurt and disappointed me. We are all broken and wounded in our own ways, and without a doubt, God has powerfully used my failures to mold me into the leader that I am today. In spite of my past issues, I am humbled that God has entrusted me to lead a ministry like CCDA and to love and nurture hundreds of men and women in our movement.

We are flawed.

We are good and gifted.

We are called to offer our gifts.

FINAL WORDS

I begin many mornings with a run through my neighborhood. I cherish this time because I get to see my community come to life. As my feet pound the streets and sidewalks of La Villita, I smile at children heading off to school, wave to merchants on 26th Street opening their shops and pray for my neighbors. As I approach the final stretch of my run, my heart fills with love for these people, just as it did when I first moved here from California.

My wife and I have stayed in La Villita for twenty-five years, and through it all I'm more convinced than ever that God keeps us here as agents of the kingdom in our barrio. Along with loving our neighbors, we take every opportunity we can to offer leadership to our community and to encourage and mentor younger leaders who are committed to working and praying for the well-being of our neighborhood.

I constantly remind these young men and women that when God gives us a burden to live and minister on the margins, he is already there and will stand by our side. I also remind them that focusing on proclamation and formation alone is not enough. Simply focusing on the demonstration of compassion is not enough. Focusing our efforts on restoration and development alone is not enough. And no matter how important confronting injustice is, that alone is not enough. Instead, if we are truly going to be agents of good news among the poor, I insist that each one of these expressions of kingdom ministry must be embraced and implemented from within the community.

In these later years of my ministry, it will bring me great joy to see a new generation of men and women from every culture and class become the Nehemiahs and Ezras who will continue the work that we began years ago. My prayer is that Christ-followers will realize that being faithful to the God of the Bible necessitates putting the poor and the marginalized at the center of our ministry activities and priorities.

If we do this, lives will change. Neighborhoods will change. God will be glorified.

This is where the cross meets the street. This is where we discover what happens when God is at the center of a neighborhood.

Que Dios los bendiga.

Seek the Peace and Welfare of the City

I am more convinced than ever of the need for Christ-followers to enter into the pain and suffering of the poor and the marginalized. In the last few weeks, American news outlets have been flooded with images of Central American children being warehoused along the US–Mexican border. At great expense and in extreme danger, these unaccompanied minors have traveled on trains and by foot across Mexico to make it to the United States. Their goal is to be retained by US border patrol officers with the hope of being given legal status by our government. The reality is that the majority of these children will be returned to their homeland to live very hard lives. While there have always been cases of children as young as seven arriving at our border without their parents, the numbers have swelled to unprecedented levels, with as many as ninety thousand children expected to be detained in 2014.

The photos of these children piled in warehouses have been shocking to Americans and are compelling reasons why our congressional leaders need to fix our broken immigration system.

In response to this crisis, thirty CCDA leaders from across the country traveled to McAllen, Texas (ground zero for this crisis), to see the situation up close. We visited a hospitality center for men, women and families who crossed into the United States without proper documentation and are now awaiting a court date with an immigration judge. After days and weeks of travel to get to El Norte, many of these individuals come to the center, operated by a Roman Catholic Church, to get their first shower in weeks, fresh clothing and a safe place to sleep. Moved by compassion, many volunteers from every denomination come to McAllen to serve at this center.

Because so much of the focus of my work has been on community development and not on relief, it was good for me to get a firsthand look at the importance of providing emergency relief in times of crisis. While I'm convinced that we need to find long-term solutions to poverty both here and in Latin America, I was reminded that emergency efforts are also desperately needed. I gained a new appreciation for those with a burden to fill this need.

In the middle of our border vision trip, we began to see another tragic drama unfold just a short distance from Chicago. In Ferguson, Missouri, a small city outside of St. Louis, a young African American man was shot and killed by a white police officer after a confrontation in the middle of the street. Though the young man was unarmed, he was shot six times. His body laid uncovered in the middle of the street for hours, creating an explosive situation.

Riots and protests followed. Conflicting reports were broadcast about the victim, Michael Brown. Cries of pain began to be expressed by African American leaders and many Americans in general. Attempts to justify the killing also began to emerge, and the racial divide in our country was once again exposed. Weeks later, much of our nation's attention is still on this largely African American community in need of love, healing and justice. My heart has been broken for Ferguson and for the despair that so many people of color are feeling in the wake of this tragedy.

In a few weeks from this writing, three thousand leaders from across the nation will come together in Raleigh, North Carolina, for our twenty-seventh annual CCDA conference. The theme for our gathering is "Flourish," and I am longing and praying that this time of collective mourning will also be a time when we can turn our anger and frustration into redemptive action that engages in the work of restoring under-resourced neighborhoods throughout our nation.

As seen by the events at our border and in Ferguson, we live in a world where the gap between those who flourish and those who do not is growing wider. Unequivocally, people of faith need to challenge our culture of self-seeking indulgence, financial disparity and racial injustice. Our vision of a just future must include the poor—the very people at the center of God's love and concern.

Since creation, God's desire is for all people and every community to flourish and experience his love, his goodness, his provision and his kingdom in all of its fullness. This is evident throughout Scripture. But the reality is that most people, families and communities fall far short of God's plans.

There are those, however, who are committed to following God's call to share life together in the hard places of this world, who hope to see God's kingdom manifested on earth as it is in heaven, who follow the instructions of the Lord in Jeremiah 29:7: "Seek the peace and welfare of the city to which I have caused you into exile. Pray to the Lord for it, because if it prospers, you too will prosper."

In order to see places like Ferguson flourish, these poor and neglected neighborhoods must become the priority of the church of Jesus Christ. Instead of driving past these neglected neighborhoods and ignoring their cries for justice and their desire to be included in our nation's prosperity, we must stop and spend time on the streets of these communities. We must invest years living and working in these communities, motivated by our love for

Jesus and for our neighbors. We must not wait for the next crisis to explode in places festering with poverty, racial unrest and inadequate educational opportunity, or where young men have a better chance of being jailed or murdered than graduating from college, getting married and finding a great job.

However, there are no quick fixes or easy solutions to the deep issues of poverty and racial injustice in our neighborhoods. There is no way to offer real hope without entering into the pain of our communities. Working from the outside rarely brings lasting change and today, more than ever, we need to embrace an incarnational approach to relating to the poor.

It's time to be willing to become agents of the kingdom, where the cross meets the street, in places like McAllen, Texas, and Ferguson, Missouri, or wherever God would have us incarnate our lives for his purposes.

May the Lord give us the burden and the courage to see what happens when God is at the center of the toughest and most vulnerable neighborhoods of our nation.

Acknowledgments

In the last twenty-five years of my life I have been blessed by working with amazing brothers and sisters in the Christian Community Development Association (CCDA) family, whose mentoring, love and support have filled my life to the brim with joy, friendship and significance as we have labored together to see God's kingdom manifested in some of the most vulnerable and yet beautiful neighborhoods imaginable. All that I have learned has been formed alongside my pastor and friend Wayne "Coach" Gordon and his wife, Anne, on the west side of Chicago. John Perkins's life and teaching have catapulted my life on a trajectory of amazing proportions, and I will forever be thankful to him for his love and support. John has continually affirmed my leadership of CCDA as a Mexican American, even though historically CCDA was birthed in the struggle of black and white relations in our nation.

I am grateful for so many wonderful partners in life and ministry: Bob Lupton, Mary Nelson, Glen Kehrein, Harold Spooner, Bill Leslie, Robert Guerrero, Rudy Carrasco, Lisa Treviño Cummins, Danny Cortes, Luis Carlo, Larry Acosta, John Liotti, Dave Clark, Leroy Barber, Jose Luis Bravo, Juanita Valdez, Ken and Judy Kalina. So many relationships from the early years of La Villita Community Church and Lawndale Community

Church along with deep friendships with members of our broader CCDA family have shaped my faith, my thinking and the way I interpret and understand the Scripture's focus on the marginalized and, in turn, the communities they live in.

It is impossible to describe the place my life partner of thirty years has played in my life. When I married Marianne, my US-born-and-bred Sicilian American beauty from Alabama of all places, I made the best decision of my life. Together, we have raised our children—Noel Luis, Stefan and Anna—with the support of our neighbors in La Villita and our extended CCDA familia throughout the nation. Without Marianne's support, encouragement and often tough love, I would not have made it through some extremely difficult seasons of ministry. Without her prayers and friendship, I am certain I would not be the man I am today. And without her lifelong commitment to walk alongside me in the barrios of Sal Sí Puedes in East San Jose and La Villita in Chicago, this book would not have been written.

Finally, I want to thank our CCDA board and staff for allowing me to take time off to complete this book. I am especially grateful for the support of Evelmyn Ivens, who helped me with research and editing for this project. I'm grateful for my assistant, Lisa Rodriguez Watson, who helped me manage my work around my writing. Jessica, Patty, Dave, Bethany, Michael, Addy, Brett, Ivan, Michelle, Amy, Aja—I love and appreciate all of you.

APPENDIX 1

A Snapshot of CCDA

In every struggling neighborhood of our nation there are fathers, mothers, sons and daughters who are striving to survive the hardships of life and are in need of restoration. These individuals and the communities where they live matter to God, and they matter to Christian Community Development Association. Over twenty-five years ago, CCDA came into existence to support Christ-followers from diverse backgrounds and denominations who are committed to ministering in the name of Christ in poor and marginalized communities. Today, we are as committed to this vision as we have ever been.

Dr. John Perkins has been our Moses for all of these years, and we are grateful for his inspirational leadership, which continues to guide us to this day. But this movement is no longer carried by any one individual or local ministry. All who are part of the extended familia of CCDA are integral to making this vision a reality. We are CCDA!

NATIONAL CONFERENCE

For the last quarter century, men and women from across the nation have gathered every year at our CCDA national conference.

To many observers our gathering resembles a family reunion more than a typical Christian event where people assemble to gain information. At our annual fall conference, we come together to connect with other leaders who understand our unique calling to live, work and raise our families in tough places. We are inspired as we listen to other grassroots Nehemiahs and Ezras who may not be household names but are living out the principles and values of Christian community development. Finally, we come together to be trained and equipped by peers and by experts in various aspects of CCD ministry. If you have never attended one of our CCDA conferences, you have missed a glimpse of what the kingdom will look like. You have also missed my morning runs, which have become a tradition over the last decade.

CCDA INSTITUTE AND IMMERSION

The CCDA Institute is the educational and training arm of our association. We offer workshops and training on the eight components of CCD. Three years ago, under the leadership of my good friend and coworker Dave Clark, we began to offer our ministry training during one week in Chicago. Participants in this immersion experience, which is attended by no more than ninety leaders, are literally immersed in our philosophy of ministry and are taught by a faculty of CCD experts and practitioners. Though this week-long training is not as flashy as our national conference, it transforms those who attend. Immersion alumni testify how this one week has revolutionized their ministries. These leaders are not only learning the principles of CCD but are also gaining the skills to implement them back home. If you and your leaders are looking for a training experience to help your community ministry efforts become more effective, this may be the most strategic investment you can make.

LEADERSHIP COHORT

Perhaps the most important initiative that we have started in CCDA in the last decade is our leadership cohort program. With the incredible leadership of my good friend and board member John Liotti, we created a space where leaders in our association between the ages of twenty-five and forty could come together and be infused with the DNA of Christian community development.

Within the last seven years we have seen over 125 young leaders participate in this program. Not only has it resulted in our cohort members forging lifelong friendships with peers committed to CCD, but it has become the pipeline to our board and to other leadership opportunities within the association. As an extension of our core commitment to indigenous leadership development, we particularly focus on seeing leaders of color strongly represented in our cohort program, but not to the exclusion of our white brothers and sisters. Because of this initiative, CCDA is primed and ready to pass the leadership baton to a new generation of men and women. Why not take the bold step of applying for a cohort?

COMMUNITY BASED ADVOCACY

In the twenty-five-year history of CCDA, our efforts at biblical justice have been championed by lifetime board member Mary Nelson. In the last five years, CCDA has ventured into the deep waters of advocating for immigration reform, initially because of my passion for the issue but increasingly with the support of our entire board and the majority of our membership. Our approach to engaging in justice issues and advocacy is unique and is marked by our CCD philosophy.

In reality, ours is a community-based advocacy approach. For decades, our members have been involved in local justice issues in their communities and neighborhoods. On a national level, we are guided by this same principle: If a policy or system is hurting or oppressing our neighbors, we must raise our voices and confront those issues.

Presently, we are committed to pursuing advocacy and policy solutions related to three key issues: immigration, mass incarceration and education. We need your voice to assure that our neighbors who are affected by these critical issues can experience true justice.

FLOURISHING NEIGHBORHOODS INITIATIVE

Fifty years ago, President Lyndon B. Johnson declared a "war on poverty," which set in motion a series of bills and acts creating programs such as Head Start, food stamps, work study, and Medicare and Medicaid. The programs initiated under Johnson brought about significant results, reducing rates of poverty and improving living standards for many of America's poor. Unfortunately, in many instances welfare programs targeted at the poor also created debilitating dependency instead of creating a lift out of poverty, which was the goal. In fact, the poverty rate has remained steady since the 1970s, and today Americans have allowed poverty to fall off the national agenda. Just think about how little we have heard about poverty in the last two presidential elections, where almost all of the focus was on the middle class and the wealthy.

While many would argue that empowering the "haves" should lead to the rising of the economic ship for everyone (including those on the margins of our economic system), the poor have been invisible in the national debate.

The church has struggled with putting those on the margins in the center of ministry and missional efforts. We have often gotten caught up in a spirit of growth and prosperity at the expense of prioritizing involvement with the poor.

Recently, President Obama established new "Promise Zones" in twenty major cities to help empower vulnerable neighborhoods by creating jobs, bettering education, improving housing and implementing other community-led efforts to create flourishing neighborhoods.

Maybe it is time for CCDA and the church to declare our own renewed commitment to address poverty in our nation and across the world. If you feel a burden for the vulnerable neighborhoods in your city, let's partner together to ensure that every neighborhood in our nation can flourish for the glory of God.

REGIONAL NETWORKS

The idea of seeing CCDA regional networks established has been on our drawing board for twenty-five years. Finally, we are ready to respond to the many requests from our members in every corner of the United States to establish official CCDA networks. Our hope is that these networks will be driven by local CCDA members who have a vision and a burden to see more effective CCD ministry become established in their cities and regions.

In the near future we envision a local network in your region that will offer you and your ministry support, training and inspiration as you implement the work of CCD in a vulnerable neighborhood. Be on the lookout for a local CCDA network near you and get plugged in.

NATIONAL OFFICE

The biggest privilege I have as the CEO of CCDA is working alongside a fantastic team. I could not be more enthused about every one of our staff. They are ready and eager to serve our members. Visit our website at www.ccda.org or give us a call at our headquarters in Chicago, but remember, we are not CCDA— you are!

Lessons from the Book of Nehemiah

EIGHTEEN IMPORTANT QUESTIONS FOR NEHEMIAH LEADERS

1. Seventy years before Nehemiah arrives in Jerusalem, Zerubbabel returns there to rebuild the Temple (with thirty to forty thousand people).

How has God been at work in your community long before you arrived?

2. Thirteen years before Nehemiah, Ezra returns to Jerusalem to revive the temple and to call the Jews to worship God.

Who are the spiritual leaders God has called to minister in your community? Who are the leaders helping people come to faith in Christ and strengthening their faith? They may be discouraged and burned out, but who are the key leaders already in the community that you can partner with?

3. Nehemiah receives word from his brother about the sorry state of Jerusalem.

How have you become aware of the needs of under-resourced communities around you that keep so many of the residents in despair?

4. Nehemiah is overcome with a burden to rebuild the walls of Jerusalem.
Has God given you a burden for vulnerable communities across our nation and world? Even though you may have known about the great needs that have existed, are you feeling a deep burden to give your life and energy to addressing the "broken walls" of a particular community?

5. Nehemiah prays and fasts for four months before approaching the king.
How has God used prayer, fasting and other spiritual disciplines to confirm in your heart that he is calling you to get involved in working to restore one of these needy communities?

6. The king sends Nehemiah to Jerusalem with resources, his blessing and political authority to rebuild the walls.
Who do you need to approach with your burden that could come alongside your work to rebuild communities? Is it your family members, your church leaders or political and business contacts? How can you get them engaged?

7. When Nehemiah arrives, he builds his own home in the city.
Like Nehemiah, are you willing to live in the community God has called you to minister in? As the called leader and catalyst of a community rebuilding effort, are you willing to take this step—to lead by example?

8. Nehemiah has to deal with apathy and with opposition from local leaders who are not concerned about the interests of Jerusalem or God's people.
Being called to the work of restoring communities is not easy and will often be filled with challenges. The most important

aspect of your work will most likely begin with helping to change people's attitudes and overcoming discouragement or apathy because of years of neglect or opposition by those in the community who benefit in some way from keeping the community as it is. Are you prepared for these type of challenges?

9. Nehemiah begins to organize the residents of the community and many Jews who live outside of the city to help with the rebuilding of the walls.

Once Nehemiah arrives and begins to cast the vision of rebuilding the walls, he has to recruit workers to get the job done. He not only organizes and deploys residents of the city, but he also uses the help of Jews living outside of the city. Nehemiah was committed to engaging both local residents and outside support, affirming them both. How can you build these kinds of partnerships with churches and organizations outside of your poor communities without causing damage?

10. The walls are rebuilt in fifty-two days in spite of many problems and opposition.

Nehemiah was able to achieve tangible results in the community, and you will need to do the same thing if you expect to gain the long-term support and confidence of the people in your community. By getting everyone to work together, Nehemiah accomplished something big—but much work remained to make Jerusalem a flourishing community. What important results are you hoping to achieve?

11. Nehemiah establishes a partnership with Ezra. He calls on Ezra to read the Torah to the people, and working together, they begin to see spiritual revival.

Nehemiah was a godly leader and was called to rebuild the walls of Jerusalem as his kingdom ministry. Nehemiah's particular assignment was not to preach or to do the job of Ezra the priest, but to complement his ministry by working to restore the physical environment of the city. By working side by side, they were both freed up to do their own jobs more effectively. Developing the spiritual lives of the people *and* rebuilding the walls of the City of Peace were absolutely necessary to bring renewal and revival. Without Nehemiah, Ezra would continue to struggle to bring about revival. With Nehemiah as his partner, great progress was made. Do you feel called to do the work of a Nehemiah or an Ezra? Is it possible for one person to carry both of these vital responsibilities?

12. Nehemiah realizes that even though the walls are restored, the ministry is not yet complete in Jerusalem.
Nehemiah was convinced that without the rebuilding of the city walls, which provided basic protection and security for the people, nothing else would change. Once the walls were rebuilt, he realized that many other issues still needed to be addressed, including the people's commitment to God. Are you prepared to stay engaged in your community for the long haul?

13. Very few Jews actually live in the city, even though the leaders live there.
An obvious problem Nehemiah faced after the walls were rebuilt was the fact that very few people lived within the city gates of Jerusalem. If the city was to be great again, he had to find a way to attract more Jews to relocate or return to Jerusalem. What is the current state of your community? Are the residents staying? Are new residents moving into the community? Is gentrification a current concern?

14. Nehemiah and the leaders devise a plan to repopulate the city. They ask the people to cast lots to identify 10 percent of the people living outside the city who will relocate in Jerusalem to bring stability and strength.

Being led by God to move into the city, these new residents built homes, started business, began new families and renewed the fabric of the entire community. The families who had never left the community needed the reinforcement of new neighbors, and the new arrivals needed the community connections with the longtime residents. Together they brought stability and strength to their community. What is your strategy to repopulate your community in a way that creates gentrification with justice?

15. Nehemiah appoints his brother governor of Judah.

Nehemiah's brother, Hanani, originally encouraged Nehemiah to return to Jerusalem, and Nehemiah trusted him completely. The work of expanding local ownership and appointing solid political leadership was absolutely necessary if all of the work they had begun was going to continue. Since Hanani was a longtime resident and had the trust of the people, he was a perfect choice to lead. Who are the indigenous leaders in your ministry who can be trusted to take leadership in your ministry and in your community?

16. After twelve years of continual work to revive the city, and after much progress, Nehemiah returns to Persia.

Nehemiah eventually had to return to Persia, as he had only asked the king for a leave of absence, not a reassignment. It is not uncommon for a leader to leave the ministry or organization for a time. Nothing will cause indigenous leaders to mature and grow like having to take responsibility for a ministry. When it goes well, it's amazing, because it shows that the vision and work can be sustained without the founding leader. But when it goes badly, it can be excruciating for everyone involved. How does this dynamic relate to your ministry setting?

17. While he is away, Nehemiah hears about numerous problems that arise with the people, especially related to their neglect of God and his ways.

After hearing about a variety of problems, Nehemiah returns to address the problems. Even though he had left, he still had a great love for the people and for Jerusalem, and he felt he could help make things right. Dealing with the reality of a returning leader has its own challenges. How are you dealing with the tensions associated with transitioning leadership?

18. Nehemiah returns to Jerusalem to continue the work of helping God's people to stay true and faithful to the one true God.

Nehemiah continued to work faithfully to make Jerusalem a flourishing city for the people and to call the people of the city to absolute faith in God. What does it mean for you to be faithful to the ministry God has called you to? How will you know if you are released to transition out of your leadership role?

NOTES

INTRODUCTION

[1]At CCDA we like to spell holistic "wholistic" to emphasize ministry to the whole person.

CHAPTER 4 BECOMING AN EVANGELICO

[1]For more on this story see "More About Our Lady of Guadalupe," *Catholic Online*, www.catholic.org/saints/saint.php?saint_id=456.

CHAPTER 5 INCARNATION

[1]Sean Freyne, *Jesus, a Jewish Galilean: A New Reading of the Jesus Story* (New York: T & T Clark, 2005), pp. 171-74.

[2]Orlando Costas, an address at a Young Life conference, Orlando, Florida, 1983.

[3]Virgilio Elizondo, *Galilean Journey: The Mexican-American Promise* (Maryknoll, NY: Orbis, 2000), p. 41.

CHAPTER 9 CONFRONTATION OF INJUSTICE

[1]I explain why we left La Villita in the conclusion.

[2]Jean Chung, "Felony Disenfranchisement: A Primer," *Sentencing Project*, April 2014, p. 5, www.sentencingproject.org/doc/publications/fd_Felony%20 Disenfranchisement%20Primer.pdf.

[3]Michelle Alexander, *The New Jim Crow: Mass Incarceration in the Age of Colorblindness* (New York: New Press, 2012), p. 141.

CHAPTER 10 *SÍ, SE PUEDE*

[1]Chris Lowery, *Pope Francis: Why He Leads the Way He Leads* (Chicago: Loyola Press, 2013), pp. 33-34.

[2]Ibid., p. 34.

GLOSSARY

abrazo. Hug

abuelita. Grandma

amigos. Friends

avenida. Avenue

Americano. Person from the United States

barrio. Latino district or neighborhood

bracero. Migrant worker

buenos dias. Good morning

campesinos. Farm workers or farmers

carne asada. Grilled meat

Chicano. A Mexican American

coyotes. Smugglers

El Norte. The North

elotes. Corn

en carne. Incarnate; in the flesh

evangelicos. Evangelicals

familia. Family

frutas. Fruit

ganas. Effort or desire

gringo. Term used to refer to white people from the United States

hermanos. Brothers

justicia. Justice

La Villita. Little Village

loco. Crazy

macho. A man who is extremely proud of his masculinity

maltratados. Mistreated

masa. Dough

menudo. Traditional Mexican soup made with beef stomach lining *mestizaje.* The creation of a new people from two preexistent peoples

mestizo. The mix of Spaniards and natives of the Americas

Mexican novela. Mexican soap opera

Morenita. The dark-skinned Mary

pachanga. A rowdy celebration or party

Paisanos. Compatriots or fellow countrymen

pan dulce. Sweet bread

pocho. Derogatory term used by Mexicans to describe Mexican Americans

pollo. Chicken

pueblito. Small town

puerco. Pork

quinceañeras. Celebration of a girl's fifteenth birthday

Sal Sí Puedes. Name of a barrio in East San Jose that means "Get out if you can"

Sí, se puede. "Yes, it is possible"

Siesta. Afternoon nap

tamales. Mexican dish made of cornmeal and filled with meats, cheese or fruit

taquerias. Taco shops

Tejano. A person from Texas of Hispanic ancestry

tía. Aunt

tigere. A ladies' man

Tío Sam. Uncle Sam

tocayo. Term used to describe two individuals who have the same first name

vacío. Empty

vato. Slang term meaning "dude"

Via Dolorosa. "Way of Suffering"; the road Jesus walked to his crucifixion

Also Available from CCDA

C|C   CHRISTIAN COMMUNITY
D|A   DEVELOPMENT ASSOCIATION

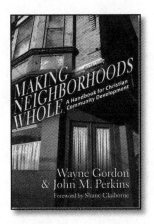

Making Neighborhoods Whole